Who Let the Blogs Out?

A Hyperconnected Peek at the World of Weblogs

Biz Stone

With a Foreword by
Wil Wheaton

ST. MARTIN'S GRIFFIN ⚜ NEW YORK

www.stmartins.com

Library of Congress Cataloging-in-Publication Data

Stone, Biz.
    Who let the blogs out? : a hyperconnected peek at the world of
Weblogs / Biz Stone.—1st St. Martin's Griffin ed.
        p. cm.
    Includes bibliographical references (page 225).
    ISBN 0-312-33000-6
    EAN 978-0312-33000-2
    1. Weblogs. I. Title.

TK5105.8884.S76 2004
006.7—dc22   2004050860

10   9   8   7   6   5   4   3   2

For Steve Snider

Contents

Where Is My Mind?

Biz Stone is to blogging what Marconi is to radio. He was one of the very first people to bring blogging to the masses—guys like me—with Xanga, and now with Blogger. Biz also interviewed me for his book *Blogging: Genius Strategies for Instant Web Content*, way back when I had just started, which made me feel cool for a few days. Biz has been doing this since the beginning, so it's only natural that he write our history.

We're at an interesting point in that history, too. Blogs and bloggers are hitting what marketers call "the tipping point." In 2003, this guy named Howard Dean wanted to run for president. When nobody in the mainstream media would let his voice be heard, he did an end run around them, and communicated directly with voters through his weblog. Within a few months, he was the Democratic front-runner. (Yearrgh!) In 2004, a Capitol Hill staffer blogged—in lurid detail—about her sexual misadventures with diplomats and congressmen. Her identity was uncovered, and she was fired, but her search for a new job didn't last long . . . she just inked a six-figure book deal. Blogs routinely pop up on blogspot.com, claiming to be "secret" celebrity blogs . . . until the massive army of keyboard monkeys in the blogosphere use their detective skills to uncover the author's real identity. In this election year, the number of political weblogs almost exceeds the number of disaffected twenty-somethings who would rather complain about a candidate's tie than enter a voting booth.

It's amazing to see where we are now, when you consider where we were just a few years ago, when I discovered my first blog . . . which wasn't even called a blog. It was just called an online diary, kept by a girl who lived in Fullerton, California.

I don't remember how I came across it, but I remember being entranced by the three years of her life that were compressed into a few days of reading online. I watched her grow from an awkward seventeen-year-old into a confident twenty-year-old. I saw friendships blossom and fall apart, I met boys she was certain she'd marry, and saw them break her heart. I watched her fight and make up with her parents, graduate from high school, and leave for college . . . and never heard from her again. Maybe she lost interest, or moved her diary to another source, but I felt a loss when this person I'd never met (nor had any intention of meeting) fell off my radar. It was as if a TV show that I'd watched for years had suddenly been canceled. I was shocked to discover that I was emotionally invested in someone I'd never met. It was like reality television . . . except that it was *real*.

When I read her last entry, I was hooked on blogs. It was still a very new phenomenon, and the signal-to-noise ratio wasn't all that good, but I spent hours separating the good stuff from the navel-gazing. While my friends and family were channel surfing, I was hitting the Open Diary, or Xanga, or Blogger, and checking in on other people's lives: The guy who worked at a big software company and talked about the difficulties he faced getting a project from alpha to beta . . . the guy who never really had anything insightful to say, but was always really funny when he said it . . . the girl who lived in Silverlake, and was always at the same indie rock shows as I . . . the guy who seemed to like all the same things I liked, even though we grew up on different sides of the country . . . all these people—real, normal, average people—were sharing their lives with anyone who cared to look. It was fascinating.

I was so drawn to blogging that when I designed my website I told my brother, "My website isn't going to be a stupid celebrity site that's just a promotional tool. It's going to be like these weblogs I read. It's going to be more like a site run by one of your friends than a site run by someone's publicist." At the time, way back in the halcyon days of 2000, no other actors had blogs, and it was kind of a novelty. These days, celebrity blogs are as common as vanity albums were in the 1970s, or talk shows were in the 1990s, but I guess I'm one of those brave pioneers who blazed the trail for all the current celebrity bloggers. (Yeah, sorry about that.)

As the blogosphere has grown and changed, a few guys have constantly been on the edge, identifying the next step, and helping us take it. Biz Stone is one of those guys. Without Biz, Evan Williams, Noah Grey, and Ben and Mena Trott, I know that I wouldn't have a weblog. In fact, I probably wouldn't be writing at all. I'd probably be dancing for nickels down in Santa Monica, singing "Buffalo Gals Won't You Come Out Tonight" while throngs of tourists did everything they could to avoid eye contact with the freak who used to be an actor.

Come to think of it, maybe I *will* head out to the pier and dance for nickels . . . that would make a great blog entry.

—WIL WHEATON

Introduction

In my home town, most of the kids grew up with Little League baseball, soccer camp, junior football, and youth basketball. Not me. Instead of sports, my mom signed me up for Boy Rangers. That's right, *Rangers*. Don't confuse Boy Rangers with Boy Scouts—we Rangers were modeled after the various tribes of the Native Americans. Sure, we learned how to tie knots and build stuff like the scouts did. But we also had to wear feathers on our head and complete a series of tests to advance from Papoose to Warrior. My name was Owlbear and I was chief of the Blackfoot Tribe for four years. I didn't play sports. Actually, I didn't even watch sports. Had to earn my wampum.

So when it came time to try out for basketball, football, or soccer at high school, I had no idea what the rules were. There were all kinds of lines painted on the field, the game seemed complex and made me nervous. I was naturally athletic—I could climb to the top of the tree in my backyard in 3.3 seconds—but I held back during the tryouts and didn't make any of the teams. Until lacrosse. There had never been a lacrosse team at my high school, but somehow the idea emerged that if we had enough volunteers, we could start a club team. I didn't know the rules of this game either, but all the other kids were just as clueless as I was. There was no reason for me to worry about all the technical aspects of the sport; the team would learn them together. Because of this freeing scenario, I was able not only to play but to succeed. By the second season, I was mysteriously great at lacrosse. They voted me captain, and I ended up the highest-scoring player. I found out later that lacrosse was invented by the Iroquois. Close enough.

In December 1999, there were already well-known individuals who had mastered both the art and science of the web. Not only did they write well about technology, but they also knew how to weave the web. They were fluent in its language and understood its rules. I was new to the web and at once interested and baffled by its strange mores.

At around this time, an experimental blogging service called Blogger was so new that it did not yet offer hosting. So I struggled for an hour trying to get Blogger to work with my two free megabytes of AOL space. Couldn't do it. I won't lie: there was cursing involved. However, I remember exactly where I was when it happened. I was on Cape Cod in the guest room of Leo and Giorgetta McRee's house, near a salt marsh in Barnstable, Massachusetts. Within minutes of starting up my clunky black PowerBook, I had signed up for a Geocities account. Back in the day, Geocities was the place to go for free web hosting. Armed with my newly acquired hosting space, I signed in to Blogger, set it to work with Geocities, composed my first post, and clicked "Publish." My life changed.

There it was, my public blog. My words published on the Web. I was a writer and a web builder. My enthusiasm for this new medium—this digital Gutenburg—was immediate. I was excited, not only for myself but for what blogging could mean. The rush of potential I was feeling translated to one thought: This is the true democratization of the web. Everybody will have a voice here. Okay, two thoughts: "Holy crap. This is easy, and it makes me look smart."

I had seen some of the early blogs. Works of HTML art combined with a seemingly endless supply of opinions and commentary on cinema, games, websites, books, and more websites. These people were masters of the web, they knew how to build it, and that's how they had earned the right to have an audience. Only their own kind could compete with their skills. However, with this new web-based software, I was able to join in. I wasn't going to be held back for technical reasons.

Owlbear successfully moved from feathers to lacrosse and I recognized the same kind of opportunity in blogging. Stepping into the world of personal publishing near its inception gave me the same free feeling. Now I could publish my thoughts, comments, essays, and ideas on the web without being a programmer or professional web geek. I didn't have to know the "rules." What compounded this feeling and really lit up my brain was the fact that this platform was open to anyone with a web connection. Sure, publishing on the web had been around for several years at this point. In fact, Geocities alone was brimming with millions of pages of pet photos, résumés, and recipes, created by thousands of amateur web enthusiasts. All of a sudden, however, someone had removed the barriers to entry and all we had to do was pour our thoughts into an empty text box and click a button to be part of the action. It wasn't going to be just a few people. This was something for the masses, and things were going to get interesting.

The more I blogged, the more I thought about blogging. I wrote articles about what blogging was, why people should blog, and how to blog better. I convinced my friends and colleagues that they should have blogs. The number of blogs on the web was growing and growing. I even helped create Xanga, a software company that provided blogging services. I was a blog freak. About two years into my blogging life, however, I started to get the feeling that something bigger was going on. My bloggy senses were tingling.

Blogging is an amazing thing, a low barrier of entry to publishing that gives everyone a voice. But from within the aggregated masses of bloggers something else was emerging. Inside the chaotic cacophony of voices, a pattern was taking shape. More than just taking shape, actually, it seemed to be coming alive. My attention split. I was still focused—obsessed even—with blogs and their potential, but I could not ignore this living network, this ecosystem that seemed to be forming.

If I was to truly understand and appreciate the significance of blogging, I had to do more than look at blogs. I would need to become a real student of this new blogging ecosystem. This study it turned out, was to be prove more amazing than my initial discoveries.

1

Who Let the Blogs Out?

L ong ago in a castle built into the side of a hill a particularly important sect of Buddhist monks lived and worked. This was not a very big castle. More like a ranch house in the world of castles, really. Still, toward the back of the castle near the mudroom was an extremely important collection of documents. Arched wooden doors opened outward to permit entrance to this room—not inward like they usually do in hallowed Buddhist temples such as this. This arrangement was by design because the room was very special. It was a repository of collected works. A library, but not just any library.

Upon entering the Room of Knowledge, visitors were

immediately confronted with an elaborate web of strings crisscrossing throughout the space. The arrangement seemed to be random; it looked like a ridiculously complex and giant game of cat's cradle. One string would go from a book high on a shelf, across the room to a scroll, once around a table leg for tension, span the distance of the floor, and stretch to the other side of the room, where a map lay open on the bottom shelf of an oak desk. From there the string would continue to thirty other manuscripts, drawings, and the occasional small statue or wood carving.

There was more than sixty thousand feet of string in the room and more giant rolls of it out in the shed waiting to be used. In the morning, sunlight would highlight the string, reflecting enough white to give the room the fluorescent glow of the future. Only monks were allowed in the room, but passersby would occasionally catch a glimpse of this illuminated enclosure from the outside and wonder if some kind of divine light was emanating from the castle. What were those monks up to in there?

They were busy creating a rustic model of an intelligent Internet. Those strings connected a passage in an arcane text to the most current map of the area mentioned within it and back to the scroll that contained the only known biography of the man who named the mountain mentioned in the text. They tied relevant selections of content together in a way that organized the information in a new, hypercontextualized way. By following the strings, young monks could study the intellectual journey of their elders and understand the interpretation of those whose initials were flagged on the strings.

Those ancient monks developed a physical manifestation of hyperlinks—the lifeblood of the web and, by extension, blogs—or they would have if they had existed. The story told of the ancient forefathers of hyperlinks is a myth. However, the point is made. Hyperlinking is rooted not in technology but in our desire to make connections, learn, and share knowledge. The world of blogging would not exist without the strands that hold it together. A glance back at some of the people involved and the events that had to happen in order for the blogging phenomenon to take place makes it seem eerily obvious that we would all one day participate in the creation and interpretation of the web.

Origins of the Hyperlink

In the 1930s visionary scientist Vannevar Bush first started writing about a machine he envisioned that would change the way we think. Bush finally wrote about the concept in an essay published in 1945 in the *Atlantic Monthly*. The essay was titled "As We May Think," and Bush called his theoretical machine the

Memex, short for memory expander. Bush's concept involved touch-sensitive monitors and a scanner. The idea was that people would store all their books, records, and communications inside the machine so they could all be accessed with "speed and flexibility." He proposed that people would use the machine to connect information in a "trail":

> When the user is building a trail, he names it, inserts the name into his code book, and taps it out on his keyboard. Before him are the two items to be joined, projected onto adjacent viewing positions. [...] The user taps a single key, and the items are permanently joined. [...] Thereafter, at any time, when one of these items is in view, the other can be instantly recalled merely by tapping a button [...] Moreover, when numerous items have been thus joined together to form a trail, they can be reviewed in turn, rapidly or slowly [...] It is exactly as though the physical items had been gathered together from widely separated sources and bound together to form a new book.

Douglas Engelbart first read "As We May Think" in a Red Cross library while stationed in the Philippines during the late 1940s. Good old Doug became an instant believer. The idea of a machine that would enhance knowledge, awareness, perception, and reasoning captivated his attention; he would later develop the basis of our current computer interfaces.

Engelbart and his colleagues at the Stanford Research Institute created the On-Line System, legendary today as the prototype of what would become hypertext. But Engelbart was focused on collaboration between people and teams distributed throughout the world. Toward this goal, Engelbart et al. ended up developing the personal computing tools we take for granted today, including hypertext linking, word processing, e-mail, a mouselike pointing device, and a windowing software environment.

Xanadu is the name of Ted Nelson's fabled hypertext and interactive multimedia program under development since the 1960s and still not finished. It's also the title of an Olivia Newton-John movie from 1980. Is there a connection? Ponder amongst yourselves.

At a time when computers were operated by punch cards, a visual environment for developing ideas was revolutionary. The concept of a "desktop" and "windows" as part of a Graphical User Interface (GUI) seems obvious now, but sixty years ago it was only for the raving minds of visionaries. Engelbart's progress influenced research at Xerox, which became the inspiration for Apple Computers. (Quite fitting because just as the Macintosh made personal computing available to everyone, so blogging opens web publishing to the masses.)

In 1960, Ted Nelson was a master's student at Harvard. Influenced by Engelbart, Nelson came up with an idea for his term project. He thought it'd be cool to build a text-handling system that would allow users to easily write, edit, undo, and save their work. Keep in mind that this was years before word processing had been invented. This project never was finished, but five years later, after presenting a paper at an annual computing conference, Nelson coined the term *hypertext*.

Ah, hypertext. How you have changed our lives. The next guy to pick up the hypertext torch and run with it was Tim Berners-Lee in the 1980s. Berners-Lee was working on a problem while consulting at a particle physics laboratory in Europe. Specifically, his task was to figure out how they could keep track of all the information in a really large project. Tim's proposal introduced the idea of linked information systems. Building on the idea of hypertext, he suggested a solution for creating, viewing, and editing documents for both individual and collective understanding.

In 1990, Tim's boss said he could go ahead with this "global hypertext system," so he started building a visual hypertext browser with a built-in editor. That way people could create documents as well as browse others. He called his project "WorldWideWeb." It's vital that we take note of the fact that Berners-Lee envisioned a system that was equal parts readable and writable—the latter part of his genius was essentially forgotten until blogging came along.

So suddenly it's 1995, and we have what we're used to

calling the World Wide Web. In the years that follow, people start building home pages and getting AOL accounts. More and more individuals and businesses get online and a world of free e-mail, portals, and online shopping is suddenly generating billion-dollar incomes and dot-com start-ups everywhere, and it becomes a whole big new economy thing. The new economy nurtures a few good ideas and smart people as well as lots of dumb ideas and lots of dumb money.

The Birth of the Blogging Industry

Blogging as we know and define it today began in 1999, when Blogger and other simple tools were released to the public. Some would say that at that time and in the few years that followed, you'd be hard pressed to call blogging an "industry" since the most popular tools were provided by tiny start-ups and usually given away for free. Add to that the fact that the majority of blogs were individual, personal efforts—not commercial endeavors and things really didn't look like they'd amount to much. Blogging now includes photos, sound, and video and is incorporated into web development, networking, enterprise systems, portal offerings, continues to exists as a stand alone service, and also creates fertile soil for ancillary products and services that feed off blogs. Today, blogging is shaping up to be a full-fledged industry but the landscape of this technology between

2000 and 2003 was still forming. Let's go back to when blogging tools were still emerging and see where their creators ended up.

Userland Software

Dave Winer is the tenacious fellow who founded Userland. Much as it is today, Userland was a small software company in 2000. Winer was a Silicon Valley veteran, well known in geeky circles for creating the MORE outliner and the Frontier scripting environment for Macintosh in the era of feathered hair—the late '80s. MORE was outlining software originally intended to be used as a simple hierarchy editor for people to plan, organize, and present ideas; and Frontier was a programming tool that Winer considered a continuation of his work with outlining. As much as he's known for his contributions to software development, Winer is known on the web well, let's go to the web and see how he's known:

Ten prominent Google search results out of about 762 with the exact phrase "dave winer is a":

> Dave Winer is a jackass
> Dave Winer is a pompous ass
> Dave Winer is still a dick
> Dave Winer is a loser
> Dave Winer an asshole
> Dave Winer is a nut
> Dave Winer is a weirdo

Dave Winer is a bastard
Dave Winer is a pretentious asshole
Dave Winer is a hypocrite

It's easy to dig up dirt like that on a well-known web personality. The results seem more fair if we use Googlism—a website that leverages Google to find out what the web "thinks" of a particular person. Here's a sampling of the many results for "dave winer":

dave winer is exhausting
dave winer is in bad taste
dave winer is one of those genius entrepreneurs
dave winer is is an arse
dave winer is a software developer
dave winer is one of the pioneers of the online weblogging community
dave winer is striding forward with his latest version of rss
dave winer is an asshole
dave winer is perhaps the single most prolific contributor to the blog community
dave winer is a loser
dave winer is insuring that he will get a lot of attention
dave winer is the villain in the story
dave winer is right up there with luminaries like tim berners
dave winer is an online legend
dave winer is one reason why a number of people have left

dave winer is a leading figure in the development of the
    internet
dave winer is maker of various nerd devices that i don't
    understand
dave winer is one of the web's best
dave winer is evil
dave winer is a fanatical blogger
dave winer is entitled to express his opinions
dave winer is dave winer

The web can be a harsh mistress. Dave Winer is a pioneer and he's as opinionated as he is outspoken. This is
very frustrating to many people—especially when you
add smart and fiery to the mix. People who try going toeto-toe with Winer (online or off) usually end up flustered
and have to walk it off. However, even his harshest critics
will not deny that Winer has made significant contributions to the success of the web.

Winer had been trying for years to figure out a way of
merging Frontier's automation capabilities for the web,
and finally, in 1999, he released a low-end content-
management system called Manila. Additionally, for
years he had been working with raw HTML to produce
his website or "hand-coding" what would come to be
known as a blog, and it had become fairly popular and
influential. Now, powered by his own content management system, Scripting News became a kind of demonstration of his software as well as a peek into his life.

Userland enhanced Manila and converted it into a robust blogging tool that could also be used to support other parts of a full website. In 2001, Winer's company released a product called Radio Userland in an effort to directly serve a growing demand for blogging. Radio is a combination of server-based software and a desktop application. The code that powers the blog editing runs on a user's personal computer. Radio automatically applies a design template to the blog and uploads it to the web when the user is connected to the Internet. The cool thing about Radio is that it ties into some centralized aggregation and tracking services. So in addition to providing blogging features, Radio allows users to subscribe to news sites or other blogs—it also automatically generates a feed for every one of its blogs, so there is a seamless flow of information to and from the web, right there in the desktop application.

Userland, at that time and now, was a full-featured blogging application. So much so in fact that it can at times be a little confusing. Users have a wide array of choices and preferences, as well as other customizable features that are very useful but at times overwhelming for the average blogger. It also costs $40 a year, which adds just enough of a hurdle to dissuade many users.

In 2002, Userland had around two thousand corporate and educational clients and somewhere near ten thousand individual users. Some of their big-name clients included Apple Computer, Motorola, the US Navy, Nokia,

I s this a sign you spend too much time in front of the computer? You're waking up in the morning and, instead of opening your eyes and looking at your alarm clock to see what time it is, you fire up Windows in your head and look in the lower-right corner.
—Evan Williams three days after launching Pyra.com.

and Harvard University, so they were doing something right. Even with a bunch of big-name companies and a large individual-user base, Userland remained a small software company and became Winer's playground for ideas and products rather than a serious knock'em dead company. In 2003, Winer stepped down from Userland and took up a fellowship at Harvard, where he stayed until June 2004, spreading the gospel of blogging, especially as it pertains to politics—with Radio Userland as the preferred tool.

Pyra Labs

Evan Williams grew up on a farm in Nebraska. Some of his primary chores as a boy were mowing vast fields, harvesting sunflower seeds, and irrigating copious quantities of corn. Those big sunflowers can get lousy with seeds. It's no wonder that he decided to found a company with the goal of making work easier.

In 1999, Williams's San Francisco–based start-up was building Pyra—online software that would help groups collaborate on projects via the web. All they were trying to do was build a project management application. Pyra would eventually be abandoned in favor of a wildly successful spinoff experiment. Userland was around at this time and so were some other blogging services like Diaryland, but they were not destined to spark the blogging revolution. Williams does, however, credit Winer as an inspiration in the creation of Blogger, as he says below in the transcript of an audioblog recording published by Noah Glass, creator of Audblog:

Hear Evan Williams yourself:

http://www.audblog.com/ media/1075/10095.mp3

> I was reading Dave Winer's Scripting News from ninety-seven on and heavily influenced by that I started publishing Evhead the blog. Being a web application developer I thought, "Well this is tedious, so I'm gonna write a script to automate this for me." That was sort of profound. When I did that, all of a sudden I could go to a web page, type in a form, and it was on my site. Arranged in this way [it] completely changed the nature of publishing a Web site. I thought, "Well that's pretty interesting." I had an Internet startup at the time and we were doing pretty much unrelated things but internally we started a blog and the people who were working with me all had personal sites and so we just basically had written the script, a very primitive version of Blogger, to automate them and we thought, "Well that's handy." And that's were the idea for Blogger was born. A few months later we actually built it on a whim.

That whim set off the blogging revolution. It also touched off some gossipy buzz when it launched because Blogger was released while Pyra cofounder Meg Hourian was visiting family near Boston. In fact, a glance at her older blog entries from 1999 reveals some archived snippiness.

> tuesday, august 24
> Blogger. (I didn't help build it.)

Buzz and gossip only fueled growth. Blogger was fun and simple to use. With it, users could publish to a website they already maintained. But if they didn't have a website, no problem—they could use Blogger's free hosting. That came a little later. A web interface for adding and editing posts plus free pre-designed templates meant users did not need to know HTML and they did not even need to own a computer, just have access to one. This meant people could frequently update a site, which was unusual given the normal hurdles for doing so. Blogger is a server-based system, which means users do not need to install anything on their own machines. Ease of use and a strong, early-to-market brand made Blogger ground zero for the blogging revolution.

Pyra Labs gave Blogger away for free, which generated huge growth but did not translate into revenue. Pyra founders thought about taking venture capital and becoming more of a corporate platform when times got lean. Offers were considered but even in the face of doom, Williams honored his instinct. After much hashing out and surely lots of weighted conversation, everyone but CEO Evan Williams left the company.

Williams was alone, but he continued to run Blogger as a free service. Not long after that, I emailed "Ev" Williams with some questions for an article I was working on. The Q and A that we exchanged in early March of 2001, not long after Pyra Labs became a one-man operation, telegraphs the decisions Williams was to make two years later.

BIZ: How did Blogger get started?

EV: We started [Pyra Labs] with some notions about better ways to manage information, both for personal and team-based project work. We were developing web-based groupware. That morphed into groupware specifically designed for web teams, for which we thought Blogger would be one simple piece. Of course, it was the simple thing that proceeded to envelop everything else. After a while, we realized that the blog thing was interesting enough to pursue in itself.

BIZ: What was the original team? How many people?

EV: Meg Hourihan and I started the company in January of 1999. Paul Bausch joined us in May, and it was just us three for the rest of that year. PB and I built and launched the original version of Blogger in about a week—legend has it—while Meg was on vacation, because she was opposed to the idea of diverging our focus. The early part of 2000, both slightly before and right after we got our seed funding, was when we added the rest of the team—which, at its peak, numbered seven.

BIZ: What was the office atmosphere like when Blogger first caught on and started growing like crazy?

EV: It was very fun. We were on top of the world, but also nervous because we knew we weren't sustainable. And for a while we were frustrated because Meg and I weren't really managers, and though we were still tiny, doubling your team tends to put some kinks in the works. We had trouble getting stuff done for a while.

BIZ: Then what happened?

EV: Essentially, we launched something sorta interesting, we got some seed funding to flesh it out, we followed the traditional Internet model of focusing on market share and user growth first, figuring we'd live off a couple rounds of financing until it made sense to focus on revenues, we got a lot of user growth and buzz and built out our technology. Then the Internet bubble burst, the second round of financing was never acquired, we failed to execute on alternative plans to generate revenue, we ran out of money, we failed around with a couple acquisition and merger deals that never came together, the rest of the team either decided or was forced to leave, I decided to stay and am currently still plugging away.

BIZ: Whose idea was it to ask user to donate money for the "Blogger Server Fund?"

EV: Probably the first person, internally, to suggest we ask for voluntary payments from our users was PB. I was never comfortable with the idea, though most of the rest of the team was encouraging it over the last couple of months. As things became more desperate, I became more open to it and finally had the idea to ask specifically for help buying new servers.

BIZ: How much did you end up making, total?

EV: We ended up with about $12,000 from users. Far beyond my expectations.

BIZ: Should blogging be free?

Ev: There seems to be a perception that we were a bunch of socialist, techno-geeks who only wanted to do things for free and that we couldn't make a business of it. I want Blogger to make money. I also want my work to reach as many people as possible. So, while I may be able to cover small costs by charging users, I think that would ultimately be severely limiting on Blogger's potential.

Biz: What are your plans for Blogger's future?

Ev: My personal plan is to continue to do interesting things that I think are important—and neat. For the foreseeable future, that means working on Blogger. My focus right now is making Blogger better, more reliable, more powerful and interesting, and importantly, financially sustainable.

Biz: What do you mean by more powerful and interesting?

Ev: By more powerful and interesting, I'm referring to some specific functionality I've been dying to build that will greatly expand the concept of what Blogger is and offer the average user a much greater ability to get their words and ideas out to a larger audience.

I see in Blogger the seed for the democratization of media, which has been talked about since the beginning of the Internet and which we have only begun to explore. I plan to get Blogger functionality in the hands of a great many more people. People are impressed by our number of users, but it's trivial.

I believe blogs will become the default format for personal home pages, which will become increasingly central to people's lives. Naturally, I'd like Blogger to continue to be the tool of choice as this happens.

Eventually, a few opportunities trickled in. Some deals—like the one with Massachusetts-based software company Trellix—generated enough revenue to keep things going and expand the operation a bit. A fee-based version of Blogger called Blogger Pro was released, and a licensing agreement with Brazilian media company Globo kicked in some cash. A growing Pyra was making money even if it was in a kind of come-what-may fashion.

Similar to Userland, Blogger was a much smaller company than they seemed to be, given their influence and the fact that they were already close to 1 million users late in 2002. The team had built back up some, they were working along, and again, they had a few different choices in terms of what direction to go in. Should they keep trucking along and bumping into revenue opportunities here and there? Should they focus on being a hosting company? What about a software provider to small business? Or maybe they should consider themselves a retail software distributor? That could make sense, seeing that they have such a powerful brand. Williams was still listening to his gut; he wasn't willing to accept the trade-offs that getting venture capital entailed. There had been acquisition talk before: maybe they would be acquired by a bigger company like Microsoft, Yahoo!, or AOL?

Acquisition by an extremely popular web company with millions of users worldwide would achieve Williams's plan to get Blogger in the hands of a great many more people. However, the thought alone would send shivers up Blogger users' spines. Blogger was the cool tool for rebels and independents. If they teamed up with some giant evil empire, users would not dig the vibe. No, the only way they could ever be acquired would be by some company that was just as beloved by users. It would have to be a company that had the street cred of a start-up with the limitless pockets of a giant corporation and a vision in line with Williams's instincts. Was there such a company?

Blogger was acquired by Google in February 2003. It was the biggest blogging news that year, and it secured a bright future for Blogger. In fact, it meant a bright future for me too, because Williams was able to swing me a job at Google later that year. So, I'd have to say that Google buying Blogger was a perfect decision. Not just for my own benefit (although that's certainly part of it), but the acquisition fits with Google's overall mission to "organize the world's information and make it universally accessible and useful." Google organizes the world's information, and Blogger helps individuals create and organize their own information. They represent both sides of a very large, globally distributed coin. Blogger, now under Google ownership, continues to be a free service.

LiveJournal

LiveJournal quietly grew on its own without much media attention in the old days. Most of its users ran personal diary sites, and the bulk of the LJ population was high school and college students. Blogger may have gotten all the hype, but LiveJournal was no slouch with the numbers, clocking in at over 1 million registered users in 2002, and more than 3.5 million registered users (and growing) in 2004.

LiveJournal is big on community and chat-oriented

tools like buddy lists of friends' blogs and various group blogging tools. For a while, growth was so fast that Brad Fitzpatrick, founder of LiveJournal, and his crew of volunteers had to implement stopgap measures. They required new users to cough up some money or get an invitation code from an existing user. Once they made some money and got some funding, however, they lifted the hurdles and allowed the growth to continue. Many old-time bloggers and industry watchers might dismiss LiveJournal because of its youthful user base. Those critics would be wise to remember another company that catered to a young audience: AOL.

A spoof site called DeadJournal sprang up to mock the popular LiveJournal. Today, even the mockery has about half a million users.

Because LiveJournal is a volunteer-run, open-source project, developers all over can create more features and enhancements as well as help out with customer service. Working on the software has become a kind of community experience, and the result is a lot of useful features that other blogging software does not have. Despite the fact that LJ is free, there are tens of thousands of users who donate to the service in the form of a paid account. So they make money.

Trellix

Founded in 1995 by Dan Bricklin, inventor of the Visicalc spreadsheet, Trellix morphed through many iterations before it jumped fleetingly into the blogging industry. First it was a kind of hypertext system, then it was a visual website building tool, a hosted small-business solution for web development, a website creation tool for partners such as Earthlink and Lycos, and finally it was acquired and quietly dismantled.

Trellix deserves mention if only because its licensing of the Blogger at a crucial time saved Pyra Labs from extinction. Bricklin had kept his own blog for years, and he watched with dismay as Pyra Labs began to disintigrate. Talks with Williams led eventually to a licensing deal between Pyra and Trellix. Bricklin would purchase a nonexclusive license of Blogger for use with its own suite of tools. However in 2002 Trellix ended up creating its own blogging application from scratch to fit in with its other features, which led many to believe Bricklin was just being a cool guy and helping out Blogger. Bricklin now runs Software Garden, a small Newton, Massachusetts—based company that sells the software he personally develops, but he has since sold Trellix to Atlanta, Georgia—based Interland Corporation, which later laid off the Trellix employees. He is, in fact, a cool guy. He helped me find my car in the parking lot at Harvard after a blogging convention. I get lost on occasion.

Six Apart

Lots of blogging tools were introduced after Pyra's Blogger, but only some of them attracted vast quantities of users. In 2001 Six Apart, a company of only two—Benjamin and Mena Trott (they're husband and wife, *not* siblings)—launched a blogging software tool called Movable Type. Very soon after its release, MT began attracting power-bloggers because the tool was laden with techie features like plug-in compatability and extensible library-driven code.

Movable Type was and remains a Unix application that requires technical savvy and special web hosting to install. It is, however, free for limited, noncommerical use. One of Movable Type's most innovative features is Trackback, which allows a blog to automatically find and republish content posted on another blog that has referred to it, thus displaying a live, two-way conversation between bloggers.

Movable Type is not a centralized blogging platform. Users must download the software and upload it to their own web server before they can access it via a browser. Be-

In just under two years, Movable Type went from being a hobby created in a spare bedroom to having gained hundreds of thousands of users, ranging from presidential candidates to daily newspapers to parents keeping in touch with kids. Next we decided to focus on bringing that same power to anyone who wanted a weblog. Today, Six Apart has five employees, and we've just launched TypePad to provide a simple, independent service to help bring the potential of weblogs and personal publishing to everyone on the Internet.

—TypePad FAQ

http://www.typepad.com/site/faq/

cause of this, it is difficult to know exactly how many people are actively using the software, but it is a good bet that the thousands of users who go through that much trouble to create their blog are active bloggers.

Movable Type is one helluva nice-looking application. The Trotts did a great job. What's more amazing is that just the two of them built it. For a couple of years, Ben and Mena made their living by selling $150 commercial licenses of MT and doing custom-design and development work as well as accepting donations from users. Then, they buckled down to create a more commercial, easier-to-use, hosted version of their award-winning software.

In 2003, the Japanese venture capital firm Neoteny, headed by Joichi Ito, one of *Time* magazine's fifty most influential people in technology, backed Six Apart, and together they lauched TypePad—a hosted version of Movable Type that made the blogging software readily available to everyone—for a monthly fee.

Xanga or "My Good Friend Jack Daniels and His Pet Zangaroo"

Ironically, before Pyra Labs abandoned their group-management software in favor of Blogger, we at Xanga were its biggest fans. We were using Pyra to manage our budding blogging software—although we didn't know we were a blogging software provider at that time. Using Pyra, the groupware, was what introduced me to Blogger. Truth be told, Xanga was not originally planned to be blogging software. We started out providing tools that enabled users to collect favorite websites, write reviews, and interact online with others in various ways. We even spent months trying to perfect a downloadable bookmark-synchronizing application called XangaSync, which never shipped. When Pyra launched Blogger and I began using it, my obsession infected colleagues at Xanga, and our tools soon morphed into a more blog-friendly feature set.

Number One Fan

I wrote about how some of these other blogging tools came about so I might as well tell you my Xanga story. It all started when Marc Ginsburg broke his ankle. It was wintertime in Massachusetts, and it was fifth grade. Marc was out playing in the snow, and Marissa Bachman slammed into him with her sled. Somehow I ended up hanging out and playing Intellevision with Marc while his ankle healed. That's going pretty far back to tell the story of a Web start-up. The point is, Marc and I became good friends. I grew up on his mom's stuffed peppers and his dad's matzo

In fifth grade, Marc threw a fun-size German chocolate bar from the kitchen to the living room, and it landed in my open palm. It was a chocolate miracle, and it was good.

ball soup. We hung out after school, we went to Nantas-
ket Beach on weekends. We spent a summer demolishing houses with shovels. Don't ask.

After high school, Marc went to Dartmouth College,
where he double-majored in Asian studies and gene-
tics, then graduated as valedictorian. In college, Marc
met John. I don't know all that much about John Hiler,
except that I owe his brother money and he has this
odd habit of falling asleep during a meal right at the
table—even out at restaurants. It might have something to do with the fact that he is insanely smart. After graduating from Dartmouth, Hiler became a
consultant and told various web heavies like AOL what
to do. After a couple years, John Hiler decided he
should stop telling other people how to run a company
and start his own.

Late in 1998 Marc and John teamed up. Marc and I
were both living in the Boston area during this time, so
we hung out and occasionally talked shop. I distinctly
remember a late-night think-tank session where we
came up with the name "Xanga." Marc, our friend Jason Yaitanes, and I were holed up in the offices of
Health Advances, a biotech consultancy that Marc
worked for after college.

There we were in these high-tech offices. The three
of us and our old buddy Jack Daniels. The goal was to
come up with a name for Marc and John's new web enterprise. We had a ton of ideas. Many were bad and
some were worse than that. The problem at this point

was that we were trying to come up with a name for a website and its parent company, but we did not yet know what it was going to be or do. We had this vague notion that it was going to be some kind of "content management" service that tied people and products together in some way, but we weren't completely clear on that. What content?

So we had nothing to go on except a list of suggested adjectives. I don't remember what they were, but I remember being told to try to think of something that suggested action, movement. One word kept coming back around. Marc had said "kangaroo." It sounded good. Maybe it was the whiskey but, hey, kangaroos are bouncy, right? Bouncing is action. Given some of the other names we were coming up with, the word *kangaroo* sounded downright compelling. Hell, a kangaroo is a damn fine example of good business, what with the jumping and the pouch and all.

During this wacky naming process, *kangaroo* was changed to *zangaroo* and *zangaroo* was shortened to *zanga*. The domain name Zanga.com was, incredibly, already taken, and the owner refused to give it up. Rather than strike up another "think tank," Marc and John decided to change the spelling to Xanga.

A few weeks later, Marc and John asked me to do some logos and branding for Xanga. When that worked out, they asked me to join them as creative director and move to Manhattan to work on Xanga full time.

Being a big fan and still a regular Blogger user, I

couldn't help but he inspired by what Williams and company had already come up with. I fought for similar features at Xanga. Additionally, we started developing youth-friendly, community-building features similar to LiveJournal, although I wasn't paying as much attention to LJ as I was to Blogger. In the beginning, Xanga's team was about six people. Xanga grew just as fast as the other popular blogging applications and it had the added benefit of built-in viral tools, such as features that made it easy to invite friends to join and others that helped you notify readers about your newest posts.

I left Xanga in 2001 when the payroll was tough and making rent in my Manhattan "one-bedroom apartment" became impossible. Enough of the team stayed on without pay to keep the ship afloat. Today, Xanga is among the top 100 most popular websites in the world, according to Alexa rankings. Marc is in the enviable position of choosing which advertisers he will allow to access the millions upon millions of affluent teens and college-age students who spend hours a day blogging at Xanga.

So What Is Blogging?

Is blogging self-expression, personal publishing, a diary, amateur journalism, the biggest disruptive technology since e-mail, an online community, alternative media, curriculum for students, a customer relations strategy, knowledge management, navel gazing, a solution to boredom, a dream job, a style of writing, e-mail to everyone, a fad, the answer to illiteracy, an online persona, social networking, résumé fodder, phonecam pictures, or something to hide from your mother? It's all of these and more.

A blog is a collection of digital content that, when examined over a period of time, exposes the intellectual soul of its author or authors. Blogging is the act of creating, composing, and publishing this content; and a blogger is the person behind the curtain. Part social software and part web building, blogging is peer-to-peer publishing—the future of our connected lives.

Legend has it that Peter Merholz coined the word *blog* when he published a side note to his website in the spring of 1999: "I've decided to pronounce the word 'weblog' as wee'-blog. Or 'blog' for short." Today, the word *blog* is in the *Oxford English Dictionary*.

E-mail is older than I am—and you know I was in fifth grade in 1984 so I'll let you do the math. The graphical web browser was introduced years after the web itself. Instant messaging was, for years, only used between paying members of private services like AOL. It takes longer than you would think, given all we hear about how fast technology and our world move, for a new technology to finally find its groove. Although blogs can be traced back to the early days of the web, they have only recently emerged as a powerful new form of publishing.

In the last five years, blogging has emerged as an important form of democratic self-expression and continues to grow in significance as the web matures and expands from computers into wireless devices and beyond. This revolutionary new form of connected nanopublishing is a deceptively simple activity. The blogs themselves are also seemingly plain to behold; yet they are as important, diverse, complex, and opinionated as the people who power them. Blogs have become popular because they provide an easy, flexible way for people to communicate that which they care about with friends, networks of friends, collegues, and broader audiences as well. Blogging software automates routine tasks and stores data, allowing the ideas and creativity of individual people to shine.

Blogging History Lesson

Depending on how old-school you are or what your web experience has been, there are various definitions of what a blog is. This is fitting, considering that blogs differ greatly in appearance, attitude, and mission. Really, what's most important about a blog is not how it is defined but the power it bestows upon its owner.

In the early days of the web, webmasters would sometimes keep a log of new pages or changes they had made to a website. This weblog would be a good place to check if you wanted to know what was new. In fact, one of the earliest pages on the Internet was a chronicle of new pages as they were uploaded. In a world where there are more web pages than stars in the universe, it's funny to imagine that not too long ago someone was able to notice every single new page as it was added.

As the web started growing too fast to keep track of everything, some of these webmaster types began using this log format in a new way. Suffering from information overload, they began to filter the web: they would link to pages or sites of particular interest and add some descriptive commentary. Their entries were arranged according to date, with the newest additions right on top.

Like pioneers, these early web geeks helped find niches among the web's formidable sprawl. Some of these old blogs still exist today. Dave Winer's Scripting News began in 1997 and still goes strong. Justin Hall's Links from the Underground, a combination of interesting links and daily diary, dates back to 1994. The old-timers can fight among themselves to figure out who was the original blogger or which is the longest-running blog. The deciding factor of what makes a blog these days is how it is maintained.

www.scripting.com—Dave Winer
www.links.net—Justin Hall

The old regime updated by hand-coding in HTML or via a custom-built management system. Either way, significant development time and know-how went into producing these frequently updated, chronologically sorted collections of personal content. These early web explorers were the predecessors to the modern blogger.

In 1999, blogging really happened. A bunch of easy blogging tools were released on the web, including Pyra Labs' Blogger and Userland's Manila. Now blogging wasn't just for people who knew how to build websites. Many popular blogs sprouted up in 1999 during the height of the famed Internet bubble.

By 2000, there was a growing number of blogs and even more blogging software, such as Movable Type, Greymatter, and many others. Hosted blogging communities like Xanga and LiveJournal also began to emerge. The number of bloggers was growing fast and jumped even higher in 2001, when blogs came into the public eye.

The terrorist attacks of September 11 were fertile soil for the whole blogging community. Television, print, and major news sites couldn't keep up with the thousands of bloggers doing original reporting, digging up links to quality information online, and adding their own voice and commentary to what was happening. There were enough blogs in 2001 to draw media attention to the phenomenon. Coverage in *Newsweek* and *The New York Times* fueled growth.

Fairly steady coverage of blogging and bloggers from then on in addition to its significant role in the new world of online political campaigning and its adoption by major web players like Google and AOL in 2003, have kept blogging on a steadily increasing popularity track. Today there are millions of blogs on every possible topic published by journalists, politicians, professors, teenagers, parents, fat people, skinny people, homeless people, dead people when someone transcribes a diary, celebrities, fools, geniuses, and probably some guy dressed up like a sultan in his onion-head hat.

On the day of the 9/11 attacks, major media websites were crippled by unusually heavy traffic, but Slashdot, the industrial-strength group blog, was churning out steady posts and holding up to the traffic. Many people discovered blogs in the days and weeks that followed.

The Three Basic Components of Blogs

There are numerous applications to blogging. However, just like a swing set, a potato, or a small remote-controlled car, blogs can be broken down into three main components. Okay, pretty much everything can be broken into three parts, but the three *significant* components of blogs are chronology, frequency, and focus.

Chronology

The quintessense of a blog is its relationship to the flow of time. In a blog, every entry or post is stamped with the date and time of its publication. Multiple entries in a day are grouped. Groupings by month are often used for archiving. It is this time-based sorting method that helps set blogs apart from other sites. Arranging the content by freshness—with the most recent post at the top—is a natural nudge in the butt for bloggers to keep adding content. Many blogs and blogging software provide search capabilities to help readers find older posts, but the emphasis is most certainly on the present, not the past. A blogger is only as good as his or her latest post.

Frequency

Blog posts are typically a few lines or one paragraph, and very active blogs feature more than one post per day. Overall, blogs are not the place for verbose, highly detailed essays or narrative features. Bloggers tend to give their readers a taste of what they're thinking right now. Something topical that relates to the here and now is more common than an extended thousand-word article. Sometimes a post could be an embedded MP3 file recorded to the blog, a video clip, just a link, or maybe a photo. Anything that captures and conveys the present. Highly active bloggers post all day long and into the night.

Focus

Blogs are saturated with the personality of their creators. Many blogs are about the day-to-day goings-on of their authors' lives, which gives them a personal focus. Others are focused on a specific topic of interest. Readers come back to the blog because they are interested in the topic or because they grow to care about the author. Even blogs that are authored by more than one person—group blogs—develop a topical voice.

f chronology, frequency, and focus are the three main ingredients of a blog, then personality is the special sauce. The greatest blogs let us peek at the person pulling the strings.

We all wear masks and a blog can hide, show, or exaggerate who a person really is. It's not a matter of creating a persona versus telling the truth about oneself, because the truth is in the posts. A blog can be an online identity that is dissimilar to the real person and sometimes it can be even more real than the real thing. In other words, someone may take a bolder stand on an issue while blogging than they would at a dinner party. They may saturate their posts with the sarcasm and zingers usually refrained from at work. No matter which direction the persona takes—closer to or further away from the real person—an identity is forged and a truth emerges in the form of a voice. This voice is legitimate, and over time it brings a kind of focus even to a blog with the most wide-ranging subject matter.

Blogs often incorporate other features, such as discussion areas, sidebar content, and other goodies, but these are not essential to the blog. Chronology, frequency, and focus give blogs something traditional web pages do not have—context. With blogs, people can create an online persona. Their blog is an ongoing exploration of that person, whether it covers their personal life or their professional interests. Blogs may lack refined editing, but they make up for it with speed and relevence.

Blogging has entered the global consciousness and is becoming essential to academia, business, pop culture, science, and politics. People are using blogs for anything from dating to organizing protests to making a living. Many blogs are personal musings. Others are collaborative endeavors based on a specific topic of shared interest. Some blogs are for fun; some are serious. Teams, families, departments, and companies use blogging as a communication tool in addition to or instead of email or instant messaging. A blog can keep everyone in the know, promote a group culture, provide the voice of a company, or lend influence and power to an individual.

> *A Blog is like an instant message to the web.*
> —*Blogger FAQ*

Webster's *New Millennium Dictionary of English* defines *weblog* as "a personal Web site that provides updated headlines and news articles of other sites that are of interest to the user, also may include journal entries, commentaries and recommendations compiled by the user; also written web log, Weblog; also called blog."

Webster's has listed "weblog" as a noun, but the popular derivative "blog" will always be more of a verb to me. Activity is fundamental. As web content finds its way into cell phones and other devices, so too do blogs cease to become "a web page." The real heart of a blog is that it represents a person—a blogger—whose thoughts, ideas, and commentary are being instant-messaged to the web as easily as they could send an e-mail.

Types of Blogs: A Bird's-Eye View

There are millions of blogs and they're all different. But when you zoom way out and take a bird's-eye view of the public blogging landscape, it's apparent that there are three loosely categorized blog genres. Most blogs will fit into one of these categories or at least have some elements that fit them. It doesn't matter whether they're mostly text, photos, video, or sound, or if they are personal, professional, or both. The three general categories are: technology, politics, and diary.

Most of the early blogs in the landscape before Blogger were technology blogs. That only made sense, since it was pretty much only geeks who were involved in the Internet in some way who had the technical savvy to develop and hand-code a blog. So back in the day most of the blogs were techie blogs with links to articles about web development or to other geeks' blogs. With all its progress, the web is still chockablock full of propeller heads so the tech-blogs are still going strong with some of the originals— like Dave Winer and Justin Hall—still at it.

Justin Hall's Web Story
My exposure to the web came from a stray newspaper in the student lounge at Swarthmore. In the December

'93 *New York Times*, John Markoff had written a piece about Mosaic and the World Wide Web. Graphics and links to traverse the Internet? The whole concept blew me away. Soon after surfing the web, I realized that nearly all of the online publishing efforts were amateur—people who knew how to use HTML but didn't necessarily have anything in particular to say. I could put my writings and words up electronically, make them look pretty, and engage the web with links. And I didn't have to pay anyone to do any of it!

In January of 1994, I read some online information on HTML, set up a copy of MacHTTP on my Powerbook 180, and put up "Justin's Home Page." The first draft had links to HTML information, some stuff about my college, a photo of me and Oliver North, a sound clip of Jane's Addiction's lead singer saying "Well I'm on acid too, and I ain't throwin' shoes at you" and a list of my favourite web sites.

Swarthmore assigned Internet connection numbers dynamically: each time my computer crashed or rebooted I had to run around my dorm getting people to restart their systems so I could be at the right place in line.

The first login from outside Swarthmore was January 23. At the time, I was a freshperson in the depths of Willets, a dorm nestled in the shrubbery of Swarthmore College in the removed pleasantness of Swarthmore, Pennsylvania. I was having a great time surfing, and I was taking the time to record my favourite links, with descriptions of the sites I was visiting. The pages grew and grew, as the web did, and as I found additional luscious links and nifty net nuggets. Soon I was paring-off pages, in order to keep my site streamlined. I decided to shift from a purely personal perspective, so "Justin's Home Page" became "Links from the Underground," after a book of dark musings by Fyodor Dostoyevsky.

My hit counts were climbing, as I was expanding my scope. Word of mouth and links from other pages were bringing visitors in, and with them comments and encouragement. Unfortunately, my enterprise was crowding the computer, slowing down the Swarthmore College Computer Society.

Since December, I had been calling *WiReD* magazine, trying to get an internship. I had met with little success; they had all the lackeys they needed. Right about the time the sysadmins at Swarthmore wanted to get rid of me, I decided to apply to work at *WiReD* online, the web page development zone for the voice of the digital revolution. I talked to Julie Petersen about the web and online and my desire to work there. When she asked for my e-mail address, I gave her instead my URL and waited nervously while she inspected my page. By the time she got to the picture of Cary Grant taking acid, she was laughing, and I had an in.

The base of operations for these pages then moved in the summer of '94 to the offices of *WiReD* magazine, where I was an online intern. Being at *WiReD* in the online department left me sitting on top of the web. *WiReD* is a clearinghouse for cool computer stuff, online and off. I did my best to keep up with the flow. Now I was a card-carrying member of their digital revolution!

Then, when *WiReD* online became *HotWired*, I was gainfully employed as an editorial assistant. As a web magazine, *HotWired* provided me with an even better view of the net. Here, I discovered that my experiences out on the web might even be worth something to somebody.

Perhaps the greatest thing about my time at *HotWired* was the people I worked with, mostly closely, Jonathan Steuer and Howard Rheingold. When both of these fellows quit, I was not going to stick around— *HotWired* was losing funsense.

I have had the opportunity to speak before groups about my experiences, and I find myself harping on one point: The web has untapped potential still. There is so much opportunity for people to craft their web wide vision. Get out there, play around, and contribute your personal effort. Take someone you know with an interesting story, and help them tell it over the web. Good telling of human stories is the best way to keep the Internet and the World Wide Web from becoming a waste vastland. With enough perseverance and personality, you could create a seminal site.

Now I have a publication that gets many tens of thousands of hits daily. I created it all on a Powerbook. It cost me nothing. I can maintain it from anywhere I can be on the Internet. And for better or for worse, no one edits me or has control over the content I provide. It is a self-publishing dream.

links.net/vita/web/story.html

A new group of blogs rose to prominence after September 11: they were called warblogs at the time but have since expanded into other issues and are now categorized as politically motivated blogs. Many of these political bloggers got their start covering the terrorist attacks and related incidents. Warblogs required constant updating and had a broad appeal. A protoblogger emerged in this category: Glen Reynolds. Reynolds's blog, Instapundit, receives well over one hundred thousand visitors per day. Political bloggers, or warbloggers, think of their blog as a personal news channel. Blogging software has become so easy and so invisible that they hardly notice it and are able instead to focus on what matters to them and their audience.

The attention these high-traffic blogs get does not go unnoticed by traditional journalism, and as a result people like Reynolds are often bombarded with requests for interviews. How do they deal with it? Simple: publish one mother of a blog post and make it mandatory reading for journalists.

Glen Reynolds's Open Blog Post to Journalists

I've been interviewed a lot by journalists lately, and I've noticed that they ask a lot of questions that don't tend to wind up in the final pieces. That's probably evidence that they're just not very interesting questions, but on the off chance that some people might be interested, here are some of them, with my answers:

How do you find time to do this?

It takes less time than people think. Much of InstaPundit gets squeezed into the cracks of the day: with always-on Internet connections at home and at work, all I need is five or ten free minutes to come up with a post. (Longer stuff, like this, is done—as this is being done—on my laptop. Right now I'm sitting in the playroom while my daughter plays with Barbie dolls.) There are a lot of wasted five-minute intervals in most people's days. I've managed to put more of mine to work. Of course, it still takes up time. My other hobbies have suffered somewhat. But that's okay. I have a lot of hobbies.

How does it feel to be a celebrity?

I wouldn't know. Being a blogger celebrity is like being a star bowler or stamp collector: you may be well-known within the group that cares about that stuff, but most people don't know who you are. Because journalists read weblogs, there's a little more crossover into the general world, but there aren't that many people who have heard of weblogs, much less any particular weblogger. It's nice, but it's nothing to get a swelled head over.

Does your wife object to your blogging?

Everyone asks that. (Would they ask a woman if her husband objected to her blogging? I doubt it.) Not too much. My wife is a forensic psychologist who writes books and op-eds, appears on TV shows, and is currently producing a documentary film. She understands about extracurricular activities.

What about your academic work? Do your colleagues like InstaPundit?

For the most part, to the extent that they're aware of it, they seem to like it. People occasionally e-mail me things that they think will be good for InstaPundit or comment that they like a particular post. My Dean has been very supportive.

Part of a law professor's job description is "public service and education." I'm supposed to write op-eds, talk to community groups and alumni, etc. InstaPundit is just that sort of thing writ large. I've got several law-review articles in the pipeline, so it's not interfering with my other writing. If it were, I guess I'd scale it back. And it's definitely helped my teaching in Internet Law—there's nothing like hands-on experience after all. It's even changed my views on some questions.

How do you find the stuff you link to?

I follow links to pages from which I follow links to others. I have a variety of places I tend to look, but I try to branch out and find new stuff. I don't want the Blogosphere to become too much of a self-referential echo-chamber, so I've been making an effort to link to sites different from mine: Christian bloggers, lefty bloggers, etc. (Some people say it's a mistake to try to drive traffic to other sites, but that's precisely what I've tried to do. I'm not trying to build an empire here, and I want to see the Blogosphere as a whole flourish.)

I also get a lot of helpful links from readers. Two of my readers, S. E. Brenner and Paul Music, are virtual one-person news services, and a lot of other readers send interesting stuff from time to time.

Do you think weblogs are having an impact on the mainstream media?

Yes. Not least because of the occasional angry e-mail from mainstream media folks who don't like what I say about them, or the more common e-mail from mainstream media folks calling attention to something they've written. That indicates that they think weblogs matter.

And you can see ideas percolating out from the blogosphere into the general world. But I think the biggest influence is just the sense that people are being watched. People write for two audiences, someone once said: the people who don't know much and the people who know a lot. Forgetting the second audience tends to make for bad writing. The blogosphere helps remind people that it's out there.

Do you think weblogs will replace mainstream media?

Probably not. I think you could aggregate weblog content to produce a decentralized version of a newspaper or magazine—a little like what Oliver Willis is doing with The American Times—but whether that will actually happen I don't know. I think that the relationship between weblogs and mainstream media is probably more symbiotic than competitive.

Do you think people will be able to make money from weblogs?

Andrew Sullivan kind of is already. I'm not—at least not on any kind of hourly-rate basis—though InstaPundit is more profitable than a lot of "mainstream" publications, which is to say it's not in the red. And if you consider the Drudge Report a weblog (something about which some people disagree), then someone already is. I don't know what he makes, but it's certainly a better living than the average journalist.

A bigger question is whether weblogs need for people to make money. I think the impulse among humans to share opinions is pretty well hardwired, meaning that as long as weblogs aren't expensive, people will happily do it at a loss. Bigshot journalists may care more about whether they can make money out of blogging, but even there I'm not sure it's all rational economic calculation. Andrew Sullivan blogged himself out of a steady gig with the *New York Times* and I doubt that made sense economically. People value being able to say what they think at a non-economic level.

What do you think will come next? Have you considered audio or video?

Yes. In fact, as soon as my audio hosting service finishes a server upgrade, I'm going to roll out InstaPundit Radio, with more-or-less weekly features of audio commentary and interviews. As for video, well, we'll see. I could offer the kind of thirty-second talking head video clips that MSNBC offers—but does anyone really care about those? I'm not sure. I might try it just for fun.

Fun is what this is all about. If I really wanted to make money, I'd be spending my time doing consulting work for liquor companies.

How do you decide which sites to add to your permalinks?
I'm not very organized about it, and I'm constantly noticing that I've left someone out that I meant to include. (I have a memory like a Ferrari: when it works it's great, but there's a lot of downtime involved.) Anybody that I find interesting is likely to be included, whether I agree with them or not. Some things that keep people off: a consistently nasty tone, lots of spelling errors, or too many emails pestering me to put them on. I don't mind being asked, but I do mind being spammed.

Why did you leave Blogger and Blogspot?
Pyra Labs and Blogger deserve a huge medal for almost single-handedly starting the blog explosion. And I found Blogger and Blogger Pro entirely adequate. Pro was somewhat more reliable, but not great. Blogspot's hosting was basically free, but also not terribly reliable:

as I write this it's been down for about eight hours. Plus, I felt (slightly) guilty about how much bandwidth I was consuming. I talked with Stacy Tabb of Sekimori, and she found me a great hosting deal and set me up with Movable Type as part of the site redesign. I wasn't actually anxious to make the move, but Blogger's reliability problems meant I wasn't opposed to it, either. Movable Type isn't perfect, but it's been much more reliable than Blogger and every bit as easy to use.

Nonetheless, I encourage people who want to start a blog to start with Blogger. It's an easy way to get started, and it's entirely adequate for most people's needs. I ran InstaPundit on a Blogger/Blogspot combination for nine months of very heavy traffic, and it worked fine. I hope that Pyra makes it big; they deserve to.

Do you think there's a feud between the older-line tech-bloggers and the newer set of "warbloggers"?

No. Some people like Nick Denton [blog publishing tycoon] have said some things along those lines. I read some techblogs—mostly Doc Searls [old-time techblogger], sometimes Dave Winer or Jason Kottke—but for the most part we have different interests. I like the techbloggers just fine, though I don't agree with everything they say on politics. And I'm sure they don't agree with what I say sometimes. Big deal. People don't have to agree on everything.

Will the blog bubble burst?

Sure. But it'll be like most Internet bubbles: the real
bubble is in attention. Napster got a lot of attention
a couple of years ago. That bubble has "burst," but
there's actually more filetrading going on now than
there was then. It's just not on the cover of news-
magazines. Similarly, someone will soon announce
that blogs are "over," but weblogging will continue
at a higher rate than it's going on now. It will just
have become part of normal life. We don't hear
much about the "electric light revolution" anymore,
but that doesn't mean we've all returned to candles.

Will you miss the attention when it's gone?

Maybe a little. But this is a hobby. I've got a life.

Diary blogs are the ones critics use as ammo against blogging and sometimes refer to as "what I had for lunch
today" blogs. The blogging communities Xanga and Live-
Journal are brimming with teenagers who have no qualms
about releasing obsessions, rants, and secrets to their blog.
The comparison between blogging and instant messaging
is apparent with these teen diary blogs. They can become
a more permanent version of instant-message spamming
their friends. Many come down on these blogs as trivial,
but they are in fact one of the most amazing facets of the
blogging phenomenon. Teenagers talk about what interests them, what's on their minds, and what issues they are
having. Xanga has a feature that allows bloggers to create
and join groups, and blogging teenagers have organized

themselves into categories for support on problems ranging from dating to self-mutilation. In some cases the most important thing is get it out in the open—even if it's only whispered to your blog.

Perhaps most famous of the diary-style blogs is "Belle de Jour: *Diary of a London Call Girl.*" From a humble blog came a book deal and a film contract. This blog made it to the big time, but is still very much like a normal diary blog, complete with the ubiquitous "ten things you should know about me"–style post. When a blog hits the big time and gets a lot of traffic, these types of posts can help fend off the avalanche of repeat questions from fans and journalists, but even diary bloggers with only a handful of readers will often publish such a list in order to create a frame of reference going forward.

Ten (Or Twelve) Things You Should Know About Belle

1. I don't plan to post a picture. Mostly because I work through an agency and don't want to cause trouble (honour amongst thieves, who knew?) This site is not to drum up business; it's just a diary.
2. I play safe. Nothing is foolproof, but I'm cleaner and more careful than most "normal" girls. Thank you for the concern, though . . .
3. Yes, I really am a call girl. A bored journaliste could probably fake this blog, but I'm not that clever. I wouldn't say no to a "real" writing career but lack the necessary perseverance.

4. My experience in the business has been more good than bad. I don't think it's for everyone but then again neither is engineering.

5. My family is quite normal, and I am in touch with my parents almost daily. They know I do "adult entertainment" and I leave it at that. On a similar subject, I am not a drug addict and have never been on the dole.

6. My ideal man is Alan Davies.

7. The Boyfriend and I have known each other years but only dated since January. He's a great lad, funny, smart, kind, sexy and the goofiest dancer I've ever met. How he controls his feelings over what I do is a mystery to me. Maybe he likes it.

8. When not profiting from my assets, I spend a lot of time reading and especially enjoy Jonathan Coe, Jeffrey Eugenides and Rick Moody.

9. At university, I studied a wholly academic humanities subject useless to the world at large. Given the choice of prostitution, temping or copywriting—the occupations in London which seem to be constantly hiring—I opted for this. Eventually.

9a. Yes, I am aware that such a career move probably indicates a lack of ingenuity or motivation on my part.

9b. But I do pay taxes, and the profession is legal after all.

10. I'll do my best to offer advice, but I'm probably no

more qualified (and a lot less experienced—in giving advice, that is) than Em and Lo. And they're funnier.

The fact that these genres even exist is a testament to the fact that blogging has already started evolving. Blogs have reacted to the needs of the world and have grown in a pattern similar to that of the web itself. At first a playground for geeks, later more popular with the emergence of web-based tools, and industry following when millions of people began flocking to the new medium.

Blogging software provides a simple, accelerated tool to get a blog published. Without knowledge of HTML or any other code, users only need to submit a form on a website to see their content transformed into a published result. Formatting and design options are performed without the blogger needing to learn a single line of code. This ease of use is what kicked off the blogging revolution. What keeps it going is the millions of bloggers who publish daily. The publishing side of the Internet has been democratized, and there's no going back. It's a little scary—but in a good way.

Blogging Case Scenarios

My friend Danah Boyd studies, seemingly, everything, but she also studies blogging and other types of sociable software. After poring over some data and mixing it together with her own field experience, Danah whipped up a kind of Frankenstein's monster—an amalgam of people stitched together to create an example of a blogger. He's not nearly as scary as I make him sound.

Meet James—The Travel Blogger

Background: 28 years old from near Newton, MA

Educational/Job: B.A. in politics at Tufts; was working as a QA at a dot-com company in Silicon Valley

Story: James got tired of his job, but didn't know what was next. To "find himself," James decided to backpack through Asia, spending one and a half years in Thailand, Cambodia, India, Indonesia, Laos, and Australia. He took massage classes, learned to scuba dive, and worked on an organic farm; mostly, he explored with other backpackers.

Blog: James created a travel blog before he started traveling. He wanted his friends to be able to stay in touch with his life. He blogged 3–4 times per week, writing about events of the day, things he'd seen, other travelers, emotions, etcetera.

Photo album: James sent rolls of film to Ofoto, which created a digital photo album for him. He would link to the Ofoto site from his blog. Photos appeared every month or so.

Travel blog community: James sometimes surfed the LJ-Travel community (a group of travel bloggers who use the Live Journal blogging software) to find other backpackers abroad. These people often made great traveling companions and were really supportive via his blog, giving him advice on where to go and how to deal with different emotions of traveling.

Audience: James's family and a few close friends read his blog daily; his mom loved that she could check in on him without "being a nag." Most of his friends read it about once a month. Only the other travelers commented; James assumed this was because they were most comfortable with the technology. His friends preferred the pictures. James figured that scanning the blog and seeing the photos allowed friends to get a quick sense of James's state; his friends often asked for more photos of James, rather than just the sights.

Conscientious communicator: Twenty-something travelers from Europe, the States, and Australia flood Asia each year. Prior to blogging, the most common way to update friends and family was via an announcement mailing list. Travelers spammed their friends and family with really long updates. James preferred to blog: "I felt less restrained in what I was writing. Writing emails can be . . . intrusive. I'd be sending it off to 100 people and I'd have to gauge if they would be interested in getting an e-mail from me every 2–3 days broadcasting that I'm still sitting on the beach. If I were to broadcast e-mails, I would do it less frequently and make whatever I write more important. It's showing up in someone's inbox and presumably most people read most things in their inbox, so it's being pushed on them as opposed to being their choice to check out my blog whenever they feel like it and if they want to scan through it or skip down and see what I am doing. It's more under their control."

Stitching together a representative of the blogging kingdom is one thing but actual bloggers are all around me all the time. So one day at work I swiveled around in my chair and asked my colleagues some basic questions to see if I could get a little closer to the reason why blogging has become so popular.

Kimmy Ho

I always feel like I should be riding a horse and carrying a sword when I say Kimmy's whole name. "Kimmy, *Ho!*" But that would be unprofessional. Kimmy works with me at Google. She knows the ins and outs of Blogger-the-application like a gondolier knows Venice. Amazingly, Kimmy works with Blogger all day long but still signs on in her free time to blog.

BIZ: How long have you been blogging?
KIMMY: Almost a year and a half.
BIZ: Why did you start blogging?
KIMMY: Some of my friends introduced it to me and I started the blog to keep them up to date on unimportant things in my life and mostly just for fun.
BIZ: What keeps you blogging?

KIMMY: I like being able to look back through my archives and see what was going on during various times. A lot of the time, I even forget that something funny or eventful happened until I reread it in my blog and think, "Oh yeah!"

BIZ: Why do you blog?

KIMMY: I blog to share events with my friends, to store links and information for future reference, document certain events, but mostly just for fun.

BIZ: What do you blog about?

KIMMY: I blog about random events, encounters, feelings . . . anything.

BIZ: How has blogging changed your life?

KIMMY: Blogging helped me to find my job.

BIZ: What is a blog?

KIMMY: A blog can be anything . . . it can be a way to communicate with friends/family, a place to store information for easy access, but more generally it is a web page that is frequently updated.

BIZ: How much does your blog reflect your personality?

KIMMY: My blog says, "Kimmy" all over it . . . in the colors of the layout, the font, the pictures, and the style of writing.

BIZ: How much time do you spend blogging?

KIMMY: I usually blog when the urge strikes or when something happens that is "blog worthy," which is usually a couple of times a week.

BIZ: How would you describe your blogging style?

KIMMY: Personal, girly, friendly, fun.

BIZ: How many people visit your blog each day?

KIMMY: 40–50.

BIZ: Is blogging work or play?

KIMMY: Play!

BIZ: Do you worry about privacy? What concerns you?

KIMMY: I enjoy that I can stay somewhat "anonymous" when online. If there is something that is really personal, I will not write it in my blog, so I do not worry too much about privacy.

BIZ: What is off-limits for blogging?

KIMMY: Very personal issues that I don't want the "world" or general public to know.

BIZ: How is blogging changing the web? Society?

KIMMY: It is allowing for people who are not "programmers" or "geeks" to start publishing to the web and to have their own space on the web. It opens people not only to blogging in general, but to all of the Internet.

Steve Jenson

As soon as I was finished with Kimmy, I turned my attention to Steve Jenson and fired off the same questions for a totally different view. If we ever hire another guy named Steve, then we will call Steve Jenson "Big Steve." Steve Jenson *is* Blogger. I don't mean he is "a blogger" (with a lowercase *b*), I mean he is the big B—the man behind the whole shebang. Evan Williams might have built the boat, but Steve Jenson is the wind. He also kind of looks like a Viking, so you see how this whole thing comes together. Steve would also want me to tell you that he's not the only engineer working on Blogger, there are plenty of other people who ~~get in his way~~ do a lot of fantastic work.

BIZ: How long have you been blogging?

STEVE: I started blogging in June 2000 originally with some software I wrote in Java, then I gave LiveJournal a try, later writing a different blogging system, then switched to Blogger.

BIZ: What do you blog about?

STEVE: Mostly technology or social issues. It has to really grab my interest or make me almost choke on my soda.

BIZ: How has blogging changed your life?

STEVE: It's tremendously useful to be able to see what other people are interested in without them having to explicitly tell you. Blogging has taken a lot of backroom conversation and has made it accessible to a whole new audience who will be able to appreciate it on other levels.

If I'm interested in something, I don't have to spend weeks digging myself into an entrenched physical network of people, of moderated mailing lists, secret IRC channels, and private dinners. Those things still exist, but many of those people blog as well.

Good bloggers tend to write to an ethereal "audience," whether or not it exists. Their posts make sense without you having to read the entire blog. We've helped create a whole generation of archivists and catalogers who are perfecting the art of writing a review.

Years down the road I can be pondering a question about some long-dead technology and I'll be sure to find some blog entries where a group of people are relating their frustration, joy, or both.

BIZ: How much does your blog reflect your personality?

STEVE: I feel that blogging is a fairly honest representation of how I see myself. It may not be what others see, but I only have one set of eyes.

BIZ: How much time do you spend blogging?

STEVE: I spend a few hours a week writing in my blogs. I spend a few hours a day reading other people's.

BIZ: How would you describe your blogging style?

STEVE: I try to be succinct and pointed. Write things down in a way that I would enjoy reading them. Some people try to make their blogging style incredibly transparent, thinking that by giving you what they consider a "raw feed" into their brain, you're going to be able to appreciate their whole being. I really don't like those kinds of blogs. I find them self-indulgent and typically boring. I like a little filter between me and other people.

BIZ: Do you worry about privacy? What concerns you?

STEVE: I don't mind people knowing about me, but I still get a bit freaked out when I first meet somebody and they say, "Oh, you're Steve. Yes, I had that same problem with that scene in that movie."

BIZ: What is off-limits for blogging?

STEVE: I don't talk too much about my private life. Also, I try not to blog something unless I think other people might find it useful. Someone might find a discussion of how I deal with knee pain to be useful. They probably wouldn't feel the same about posts occurring every half hour where I proclaimed eternal hatred for my knee joints and a subsequent post apologizing to my knees. I wouldn't want to read that.

BIZ: How is blogging changing the web? Society?

STEVE: Something I really appreciate about blogging is how it has focused the web away from being a billboard for crappy products and instead has turned it into a canvas for a group mural. Some pieces are very practical and some very abstract.

2

Blog This! A Cultural Style Guide

```
javascript:Q=";x=document;y=window;if(x.sel
ection){Q=x.selection.createRange().text;}-
else%20if(y.getSelection){Q=y.getSelection
();}else%20if(x.getSelection){Q=x.getSelec-
tion();}void(window.open('http://new.blog-
ger.com/blog_this.pyra?t='+escape(Q);+'&u=
'+escape(location.href)+'&n='+escape
(document.title),'bloggerForm','scrollbars=
no,width=475,height=300,top=175,left=75,sta-
tus=yes,resizable=yes'));
```

Above is the code for a tiny application that is responsible, in large part, for the rise of blogging culture. BlogThis! is a software program that runs in the URL field of a browser—the place where you usually type the web address you want to go to. It looks just like a regular hyperlink, but when you drag it to your toolbar, it becomes a mini blogging application. When clicked, this mini application pops up in a little window preloaded with a link to the web page you are visiting as well as any text you have highlighted on that page. In other words, if you're surfing around and you find something interesting, then you just click BlogThis!, add your thoughts, and click an update button—you have just updated your blog with your thoughts on that web page.

I am told that when they built the University of California at Irvine, they did not put in any sidewalks the first year. Next year they came back and looked at where all the cow trails were in the grass and put the sidewalks there. —Larry Wall, Programmer

http://www.softpanorama .org/People/Wall/larry_wall _articles_and_interviews .shtml

Late in 2003, Google added a BlogThis! button to version 2.0, the popular Google toolbar application, introducing blogging to millions overnight. BlogThis! provides a deceptively simple interface for what is really just the tip of the blogging iceberg. Blogging, although simple, is lousy with subtle cultural idiosyncrasies. Like bees communicating through dance, or a traditional Japanese tea ceremony, Bloggers have invented an array of customs, implied rules, and tacit regulations. The world of blogging operates in interesting ways and to the degree you choose to play along, you have more or less control of your own sphere of influence in and impact on the medium.

Nobody chiseled the commandments of blogging into stone tablets and decreed them to be followed to the letter. In fact, the rules of engagement in the world of blogs have emerged from the bottom up.

Blogging Etiquette

Blogging is the Wild West of publishing—a place where everyone gets unlimited ammo as long as they have something to say. This first real democratization of the Internet is a social revolution, and it's not always pretty. The blogging phenomenon, like the web itself, grew from grass roots. Blogger, launched almost by mistake in 1999 as an internal side-project, exploded into the biggest development on the web since ~~Al Gore~~ Tim Berners-Lee invented it.

Blogging really is as easy as sending an instant message to the web. This ease of use is part of why it has grown so popular. We can't blame bloggers for occasionally being a little rough around the edges; it's just too easy to fire off a few angry sentences. Anyone who has ever used e-mail knows that. Nevertheless, we now have about five years of experience from which to garner a few guidelines to proper blogging etiquette.

You Are What You Blog

Starting a new blog is simple. In three painless steps—"create," "name," and "choose"—you have a publishing platform and an audience of hungry readers waiting for your pithy posts. For many, blogging is a foray into the world of broadcasting. For the first time, these otherwise unknown individuals are releasing personal ideas and opinions to the general public. They are sharing a unique voice and inviting a potential audience of millions to experience their personality. For others, blogging is a secondary way to reach an audience. Perhaps they already have experience with mailing lists or message boards. In some cases seasoned newspaper, magazine, and television journalists have turned to blogging as a more direct, low-barrier broadcasting medium. Journalists bring their own set of ethics and guidelines to blogging, but they still need to learn the house rules of the blogosphere.

In any case, there are many ways to screw things up. As luck would have it, I have already made several of these mistakes. Allow me to relay this knowledge to you, gentle reader, so that suffering and pain may be minimized. Remember that your blog is an extension of yourself. It is a web proxy, a version of you online. You are what you blog, so you can't really protest, "I never said that!" because, well, it's right there on the screen.

Better Blogging: Finding Your Voice

Most bloggers value links and traffic to their blog. If you have 20 visitors a day, you want 50. If you have 50, you want 100. Madness can ensue. Keep in mind that a good blog—that is, a blog with good information, links, and a memorable voice—will draw attention and hold it. Your visitors will return if you keep them in mind. Blogging for maximum popularity in the blogosphere can lead you down the wrong path.

Do not allow yourself to be overly self-conscious about what you choose to feature in your blog. "Will people think this link is interesting? Will I seem like a geek if I point out that the pagination in my Star Trek Technical Manual is off by a number that is divisible by pi?" These sorts of questions should not keep you from blogging. You are also blogging for yourself. If you find something worth linking and discussing, then go ahead and publish it. That's good stuff. (Incidentally, the answer is yes. People will think you are a geek if you post that Star Trek thing. But remember, in the blogosphere, geeks are cool.)

If you need to give yourself some lines to color within, that is, if you want some way to maintain quality control, it's best to keep in mind a core group of readers as you blog. This group will act as your beacon and keep your blogging on track. It will also help you keep your blog voice authentic. Who are you blogging for? A few friends? Your grandparents? Colleagues? Think of a particular person or group when you create your entries, but bear in mind that a wider audience could also be reading. So take care not to get too personal or specific—don't let your blog turn into a series of inside jokes. An inside joke once in a while is fun but beyond that is a turnoff.

While I'm on the subject of going crazy, please remember this: Don't blog drunk. Blogging is easy; you type in a box and click "Publish." Not to mention that, with various enhancements, your posts can be automatically e-mailed directly to hundreds of friends and colleagues. Great technology. However—and I can't repeat this enough—not when you've lost the ability to reason.

You'll understand what makes blogging tick after you've actively tried it for a few months. Here are a few tricks of the trade you're most likely to discover. Recognize them early so you can get up-to-speed that much faster. Then you can focus on coming up with your own, unique tricks of the blogging trade.

Find your voice. Blogs are used to keep in touch with friends, establish a reputation, get politicians elected, market products, preach religion, record personal life events, and for a thousand other things. Discovering your blog persona will help you stay focused and keep you on track. Finding your blog voice is most effectively done by keeping at it for six months to a year.

Work the room. You should keep in mind who you are

Many bloggers feel the need to warn their audience when they think posting will be light due to some real-life business cutting into blogging time. Oddly, this is often followed by prolific posting.

blogging for. Is it a group of friends? Academic colleagues? Customers, strangers, or just yourself? Keeping your readers in mind will help you develop a consistent blogging style. In this way, your blog persona becomes a kind of memorable brand that readers will want to visit again and again.

Say "no" to mumbo jumbo. Strive to keep your posts authentic. Don't write like a late-night infomercial even if you are a marketing professional. It's best to write like a real person about real stuff.

Stay on passion. Blog about something that really interests you and infect every post with attitude and opinion. Don't write about something you're not really that interested in because you think people will want to read it, and don't curb your enthusiasm for fear you will sound crazy. Crazy is good. Let us have it and you'll stand out.

Keep 'em coming. When you start a blog, you make a deal with your initial readership: You keep posting new stuff, and they will keep coming back to read it. Some bloggers post several times a day, some just once a day, and others a few times a week. Think of it like working out: you can't just do it once in a while; it doesn't work that way. You have to work blogging into your lifestyle, and you have to keep at it. At least three or four times per week, minimum.

Don't be an ass. It's still the wild web out there, so you're not going to be blacklisted if you copy and paste some text here and there or if you get a bunch of great links from another blogger. But put some quotes around it—italics, something. Don't make like you wrote it straight up. And link back to somebody if you found something weird or cool from them. You're better off doing that anyway because links are the currency of the blogosphere. Crediting your sources makes you look more legit and builds a better network of information.

Relax. If you post frequently, stay interested, and have fun, then your readership will grow over time. Don't stress out about getting more hits or if some bloggers link to you and call you a twit. Keep at it and watch your audience build gradually. Definitely check your stats and react accordingly, but don't blog only for hits; it won't work out in the long run, because any repeat visitors worth having are going to smell desperation a mile away.

Blogging and Your Privacy

Now might be a good time to reiterate that blogs are available to a public audience just as television, newspapers, and radio are. When you publish a blog entry, you are broadcasting information to a potential audience of millions.

There are many people who, for some strange reason, think they know exactly who is and who isn't reading their public blog. This may be partially true via the protected posting features of some blogging applications, but most of the time it is not. It is odd to think that people would get upset to learn that their blog, which they know to be a publicly accessible document on the Internet, is being read by people they have not personally invited. That's what makes blogging great. However, there are times when people prefer to protect their identity a little bit. Especially when it comes to school or work. There are a few commonsense precautions you can take to make your blog less obvious to your employer or your teacher. A little self editing goes a long way, but if you think you may occasionally slipup here are a few things you can try.

> **Geek Tip:** You can keep search engines from indexing your blog if you put this bit of code in your template's <head> area:

```
<META name="ROBOTS" content="NOINDEX,
NOFOLLOW" />
```

Get out the coleslaw and find a nice patch of lawn, because I'm about to roll out a blanket statement: If it is on the Internet, it is not private. When you publish text, images, audio, or any other kind of document to the Internet, it is immediately viewable by the world. If you have a stalker, don't publish your address and phone number. If you are planning to defraud your former employer with false back-injury claims, don't blog about the break-dancing trophy you won last night at Club Scam.

When it comes to blogging and the privacy of others, be sensitive to conversations or messages that they might consider "off the record." Blog unto others, and all that.

Although it is often possible to mark your blog posts as "private," do not write something in your blog that you never, ever want anyone to read. If it is super private, you shouldn't be submitting it to the Internet, even if you are not making it public. Many people have taken to using blogs as online diaries, but please don't get too carried away with this idea if you are not comfortable with the possibility of someone reading it. Don't publish personal information to the web and think your boss will not read it because "she doesn't read blogs." Bad move.

If you're sensitive about people spotting your blog, then be careful. It only takes one "meddling kid" to foil your schemes.

A friend of mine got into a little snafu with a coworker when he linked to his blog. The guy had taken care not to put his name anywhere on his blog and had posted a bit of text requesting that anyone who wanted to link to his blog should first ask for permission. When my friend linked to this guy's blog without permission using his name as the link, the guy felt as though he had been "outed" and deleted his entire blog.

It is unreasonable to make the kind of requests this guy was making; you cannot hide a blog forever, and people link to sites on the web—that's how it works. You should know this before you start your blog. If you want to keep it private, don't tell anyone about it or, even better, don't make it a public blog.

Terms of Service

Different blogging providers have different policies. If you use a blogging provider that also hosts your blog, it's important to make sure that you own your content and that the provider only has a license to rebroadcast your work on the website. This is usually standard.

Some people get a little nervous when they read terms of user documents—especially professional writers who earn a living with their words. For example, this snippet from Microsoft's blogging service, The Spoke, might make someone nervous:

> However, by posting, uploading, inputting, providing or submitting ("Posting") your Submission you are granting Microsoft, its affiliated companies and necessary subli- censees permission to use your Submission in connection

with the operation of their Internet businesses (including, without limitation, all Microsoft Services), including, without limitation, the license rights to: copy, distribute, transmit, publicly display, publicly perform, reproduce, edit, translate and reformat your Submission; to publish your name in connection with your Submission; and the right to sublicense such rights to any supplier of the Services. No compensation will be paid with respect to the use of your Submission, as provided herein.

You, not they, should own your work. Just as you are responsible for what you publish—not them. If you're unclear of what your blog provider's TOS is, visit the welcome or home page of the site and scroll to the bottom. There you can often find a link that says "terms of use" or "terms of service."

Secret Blogging

Some blogging providers offer password protection, some offer the ability to allow only specified members of a community to view your blog, and some offer no form of privacy protection whatsoever. Nothing is guaranteed to be private. You're better off maintaining a public blog and avoiding publishing content that you cannot own up to. Still, if you want to lower the chances of your friends, coworkers, or the world at large "discovering" your blog and you don't have any fancy password-protection savvy, there are a few low-tech ways you can separate your church from your state.

I've heard of people using a different blogging application than they normally would when they want to post ultrasensitive material. Theoretically, this will throw people off because if they know you're a Blogger user, they would never believe that you have a Userland account. If you do this, *don't* link to your other blog. Duh.

You're going to have to fight the urge to design yourself a killer secret template. You must prevail. Use a default template design that comes with the blogging application. Don't whip something up in your signature style. The goal is to remain incognito, and it would be easy for your friends to recognize your design.

Are you comfortable with your sexuality? Good, now change your sex. It may feel weird, but just go with it. If you're a girl, pick a template that a guy would pick and vice versa. Do the same thing when you're referring to people in your blog, try writing "she" instead of "he." You may also want to consider signing up for a free e-mail account somewhere in the same way, just in case you need e-mail to set up any blog add-ons like a blogroll (your list of favorites) or a site meter (a hit counter).

Don't link to your real blog. Why do I have to keep telling you this? If you link to your other blog, suspicion will be aroused. Coworkers and friends are smarter than you think. Also, don't do your blogging on both blogs at the same time every day. In the event that somebody is on to you and checking both blogs, he or she might start to recognize a pattern.

Ah yes, patterns. That's another thing. If you have a certain way of titling your posts or blogging links, switch it up a little. Create a secret style so readers won't be able to recognize your usual modus operandi. Does this sound paranoid? Yes it does, but you're the one who's obsessed with secret blogging, not me.

Be careful with various blogging extras such as syndication. If you have turned on an Atom feed for your blog so people can read your posts in their favorite newsreader application, be sure that your identity is not associated with that feed. Test it out before you make it public.

Here's a tip: find an anonymous blogging provider such as Invisiblog:

> Unlike other blogging and hosting services, Invisiblog doesn't have access to any potentially sensitive information about you—not even your email or IP address. All contact between bloggers and invisiblog.com is via the Mixmaster anonymous remailer network, which uses encryption and "mixnet" techniques to hide the source of an email. We can't reveal your name or IP address—not even accidentally, or at gunpoint, or under a court order—because we simply don't have that information.
>
> —From Invisiblog's Frequently Asked
> Questions (FAQ) Page

Blogging Scenario: What to Do When Your Mom Discovers Your Blog

With the raw materials in my blog, [my mom]
could actually construct an accurate picture of
who I am. This is fucking serious. —The Onion

You will need to be prepared in the event that your secret blogging techniques go awry. A popular scenario is the "Mom Discovers Blog" situation. Do you blog about stuff that you would never tell your mom? Think about that for a minute. Deleting your blog and abandoning your loyal readers is a last resort and should only be undertaken under dire circumstances. Here's a list of suggestions to help your navigate around the dreaded Mom scenario (or prevent it altogether).

Use a Pseudonym

Join the prestigious ranks of literary superstars like Samuel Langhorne Clemens (Mark Twain) and Eric Arthur Blair (George Orwell) who, just like you, required pen names to keep their moms blissfully cloaked in ignorance. To do this, edit your user profile and change your name. If you make an alias out of your pet's name and the street you grew up on (for me: Bruce Upwey), your mom will probably see right through it. Be creative.

Change Your Blog Address, Keep Your Readers

This method will only work on moms who are dazzled into confusion by the word *subdomain*, but it's worth a try. If you change the URL of your hosted account, the old address will remain. Simply post "My new subdomain is 'nomom'" (or some such) before you switch your subdomain name. Your regular readers will know to type "nomom.blogspot.com," but you will have thrown the person who gave you life into frustration and confusion. Good work.

Search and Modify

Censorship is generally thought of as a negative thing, but in the blogosphere it can be useful. You know how faces are sometimes digitized or blurred on reality and news programs to obscure people's identities? You can go that same route with your blog by searching for potentially incriminating keywords and editing for a softer, more mom-friendly vocabulary. For example: "I got really drunk last night." becomes, "I got really marshmallow last night." It may not make sense, but it does give you plausible deniability, which could help. Every little bit counts.

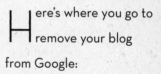

Here's where you go to remove your blog from Google:

http://www.google.com/remove.html

The Disclaimer

Another good way to dupe your mom? Include a disclaimer on your blog. Prescient blogger Tony Pierce claims "nothing in here is true." Feel free to write your own disclaimer and include it as a permanent part of your blog's template. Just tell your mom that your blog is an experiment in fiction and she need not worry. If you choose this technique, be careful not to blur your own understanding of the difference between fiction and reality. That could lead to even bigger problems.

Go to the Source

Like most of the world, your mom may use Google to find your blog in the first place. If you suspect this is the case, you have an option. You can remove your blog from Google so that your mom (and others) cannot find it. Of course, this move keeps out more than just your mom, so think about it first. Every mom is a different case.

I love my mom as much as you do yours. I also strive to understand the needs and concerns of all bloggers in these complex times. Be nice to your mom and call her at least once a week. Take her out to lunch once in a while; show some respect. And most important, don't give her more to worry about than she already has—if that means steering her gently away from your blog, so be it. I'm here to help.

Blogging off the Company Pier

Moms are one thing. Bosses are an entirely different story. Ideally, a company will respect your right to express yourself personally through the format of a blog. If you are going to identify yourself as a company employee, or if you plan to blog about subjects related to your company's technology or business, keep in mind that your readers will view you as a representative of the company—whether you are or not. With that in mind, the following are some guidelines to keep you out of trouble.

- Make it clear that the views expressed on your blog are yours and yours alone. Place this disclaimer prominently: "The opinions expressed in this blog are my own and do not reflect those of my employer."
- Be careful not to disclose any confidential or proprietary information. Read your company's confidentiality policy to find out what is considered confidential.
- Strive to be respectful of your company, coworkers, customers, partners, affiliates, and even competitors. (Even if you delete it, Google saves it!)
- Note that once a post out there—even if you delete it—it can be out of your control. People can take screenshots of your blog and search engines like Yahoo! and Google copy and save websites and make

them available to people (that's what the link that says "cached" means).

- Use company logos or trademarks on your blog only with permission.
- If your company asks you to suspend your blogging activities to ensure compliance with securities regulations or other laws, be reasonable.
- Let someone in your company, preferably your boss, know about your blog as early as you can even if you only briefly mention work-related anecdotes. Don't let them "discover" your blog on their own.

Blogging can be a serious, life-altering experience. So can getting fired. If you find yourself blogging at work and checking your referrer logs and surfing the blogosphere and starting to think it might make a great post if you made fun of one of your coworkers, then you need a little reining in.

These days, many companies are blog-friendly because they recognize a valuable tool for communicating and sharing ideas when they see it. However, as with any public medium, care should be exercised. Fret not gentle blogger, I've put some thought into this to help you keep those paychecks rolling in.

There are many ways of causing trouble at work and eventually getting fired. This is as true of blogging as it is of sending an e-mail, getting drunk at a company party, or just plain old-fashioned doing a really bad job. A hapless Microsoft employee was a straight-up sacked for posting a photo to his blog. This, in and of itself, is not so bad. In fact, a photo makes a fine blog post.

If this unfortunate blogger had merely posted an image and not also published additional information that helped to describe the private geography of the corporate campus, his sacking night have been avoided. Just because you have information does not mean you should release it to the entire wired world. Also, having a job and keeping a blog on the side without first telling your bosses is dangerous. It's more shocking when they "discover" your blog one day and is more likely to lead to a negative situation. It doesn't help if you're already skating on thin ice, my friend. Yeah, I'm talking to you. It wouldn't hurt to be on time once in a while. Jeez.

Look, I know you can't work *all* day. In fact, a healthy dose of intellectual distraction is necessary for productivity. According to me. Who knows, there may even be statistics that prove two hours of actual work per day is enough to keep the world running smoothly. Nevertheless, a traditional boss will want to see you working, not blogging, when he or she visits your cube. Unless blogging is part of your job. If your blogging is not overt there is less chance of being spotted in the act. Try to use shortcuts; if your blogging provider of choice offers one, a blogging bookmarklet is the way to go: it's a fast little window for blogging on the fly.

Remember that your blog posts are arranged by date and time. So it is very easy for anyone reading your blog to discover that you were posting at 10:23 A.M. on Monday when you were supposed to working on your TPS report. The solution is fairly easy: change your publishing schedule. Most blogging applications will allow you to create a draft and then publish it a later time. Perhaps when you are at home.

If you think your employer might be blog-friendly, you could take preemptive actions to stave off getting "blogcanned." Try asking if your company has a blogging policy and then adhere to it. Or, meet with your boss to find out if it's okay to blog.

Give your bosses a clue. If you work for a company trapped under the cadaverous thumb of an arcane corporate policy of business-speak and double-talk, you may need to modify the intellectual environment of your workplace before even suggesting a blogging policy. This can be daunting, but *The Cluetrain Manifesto: The End of Business as Usual* by Christopher Locke, Rick Levine, Doc Searls, and David Weinberger will help. Dig up a copy of this book or print it out from the web and leave it on your boss's desk. Put a sticky note on page 39 where it says:

> *This fervid desire for the Web bespeaks a longing so intense that it can only be understood as spiritual. A longing indicates that something is missing in our lives. What is missing is the*

sound of the human voice. —The Cluetrain
Manifesto: The End of Business as Usual

Bloggers tend to be smarter than ordinary citizens. After all, writing on a daily basis forces you to think, and typing does require some hand-eye coordination. If you end up getting yourself fired for blogging, I have to think that in some way, you wanted out of that job. Take the case of Heather B. Armstrong and her blog, Dooce.com. Heather has a great blog—it's beautifully designed and well written. She is an intelligent and sophisticated woman, yet Heather did not adhere to any guidelines pertaining to the mixing of blogging and work—except perhaps her own warped idea of what was acceptable. In fact, she seemed to be inviting trouble. An example is Heather's lengthy post entitled "The Proper Way to Hate a Job" with her key suggestions summarized below.

- Wear the same shirt and jeans you passed out in the previous night
- Exercise your right not to shower
- Arrive an hour late to work singing "Smack My Bitch Up"
- Take a two-hour lunch: one hour for the burrito, one hour for the nap
- Spend the rest of the afternoon downloading music; specifically multiple copies of "Get Ur Freak On"
- Avoid work all day; leave early

Remember that Heather's was and still is a popular and therefore considerably well-visited public blog and the number one Google search result for the query "Heather Armstrong." So it would be very easy for any one of her coworkers to "Google her" any time. Here's another jewel of a tip from that very same blog post—this may have been the straw that broke her bosses' back.

> Ignore the inane string of email from the Vice President of Spin to the Vice President of Enabling His Fist Up Your Ass, cc'd to everyone in the company because, really, what's a cock fight without an audience? Instant message the only other cool person in the office—the only other person who's not wearing a belt that matches his shoes—to tell him that Her Wretchedness is once again ordering Prada shoes online and talking about it out loud.

It was no surprise when, about a month after that post, Heather published another entry to her blog entitled "Collecting Unemployment." She knew she had gone too far and expressed as much by writing, "I made my bed; I'll lie in it," but Heather still felt as if her own personal blogging code should have been good enough for her employers.

> I defended myself rather studiously, explaining that I had never mentioned the company or any employee by name,

and that I had exaggerated several characteristics of the personalities showcased in a few of my posts.

When she went on to explain how her blog came to be read by her bosses it became evident that Heather felt betrayed and was more than a little bitter about the way things had gone down.

> Two weeks ago an anonymous person emailed every vice president of my company to inform them that I had written unsavory things on my personal website . . . If you're going to be a whistle-blower, for God's sake, don't be a coward about it. Fess up, you motherfucker.

Once she had vented a little, Heather proposed a few questions to her readers. She knew how she felt but she wanted to tap in to the wisdom of blogs. Presumably, she wanted to find out if she had been wronged or was just plain wrong. The questions she posited to the blogosphere essentially boiled down to two issues:

1. Is she accountable by her employer for what she has published on her blog even if she was careful not to mention specifics?
2. Would it be different if the "whistle-blower" turned in a notepad on which she had scribbled the same content?

Heather's perception of her blog is fundamentally flawed. She runs into trouble when she compares a blog to a handwritten note. On her blog, Heather published her thoughts and opinions for the world to read. That is not the same as a few sentences scrawled on a pad and intended to be a private exorcism of emotion. A blog is a published work available to everyone in the world.

In addition, Heather referred to the person who discovered her blog as a "whistle-blower." A public blog with your name all over it should not be thought of as a secret endeavor that you fear someone you know will discover. In fact—with the exception of a surprise party—secret endeavors that you fear friends or colleagues could catch you doing and rat you out on are generally not a good idea. The same goes for blogs.

Part of Heather's problem was the way in which her boss found out about her blog. If Heather had made Dooce.com public knowledge from the beginning and her coworkers had been able to follow along, to understand subtle references and match them with the person they know and work with, then the "whistle-blowing" aspect of the discovery may have been avoided.

Instead, Heather's colleagues were introduced to the blog cold. It's like when you turn on the radio three-quarters of the way through a song: you've missed the buildup and gone straight to the crescendo. (Whoa. That's an annoying song.) Heather's coworkers had no context, so they were unhappily surprised when they finally tuned in and realized they were being used as material on a personal website—as if they were starring in a reality show without consent.

Please remember that blog posts are usually date and time stamped by default. If your boss or colleagues tune into your blog, they will be able to read the five-hundred-word rant about the movie you saw last night. No big deal unless you were supposed to be in a meeting at the same time your movie review was posted. Or if there are eight verbose posts scattered throughout the day and none of them are during your lunch break. The hard chronological truth aspect of blogging will shine its light on your slacker ways.

Good Linking Habits

Links are the currency of the blogosphere. Every time another blogger links to you, your blog becomes more "valuable." If a popular blogger links to you, traffic to your blog will increase dramatically for a short time. Even after the drama dies down, you may find that your daily traffic has increased overall because so many new visitors were introduced to your work.

Most bloggers have installed or activated some way to monitor the

Blogging Tip: When crediting the blog where you discovered your post fodder, you should honor the original blogger with a link. Example:
<a href=
"http://www.biz
stone.com"> Via
Biz Stone</a>

Search for the "cosmos" of any page, and Technorati lists every other page that has linked to it in the past twenty-four hours, ranked by freshness or authority. It shows the contextual text surrounding the inbound link, its age, and other helpful facts.

number of visits to their blog and where those visitors come from. This information is called "referrals." Some bloggers check these stats once a week; others click "Refresh" on their browser so they can monitor them by the minute. Someone once even hacked AOL's Instant Messenger so that it would IM him whenever someone visited his blog. He called the hack "Instant Gratification." Checking stats is so much a part of blogging that some services have sprung up around it. A site called Technorati allows bloggers to view their "link cosmos." It's similar to referrals. The basic idea is to see who's linking to you and what they're saying when they do it. Checking this information once or twice a day is okay because it's fun to discover new bloggers linking to you and talking about you. But don't let it spiral out of control. This "link lust" can lead toward desperately linking to anything you think might be popular instead of something you actually found interesting or relevant.

Because links increase the value and popularity of a blog, people have been known to misbehave when it comes to getting them. Should you find that you are developing an insatiable appetite for "linky love" to the point that you are beginning to dream up schemes for getting more bloggers to link to you, then you are becoming dangerously close to what bloggers call a "link whore." Excuse my French. Not a good reputation to have, especially when you're just starting out. Take for example, this blog post from William Hooker (no pun intended):

> A Blogger's Creed: I believe that there is no length too far to go for more blog traffic. Silly contests, made-up awards, even kissing up to other bloggers are acceptable, so long as it increases my post count by at least one. —William Hooker
>
> Source: http://trojanhorseshoes.blogfodder.net/

William has the wrong idea. While creative ideas for drumming up traffic are a good idea, schemes are not. Don't scheme in ways that are insidious; don't be a spammer for more traffic. Blog frequently and blog well. You will see an increase in your readership over time and you will be able to point to quality archives.

Beyond just plain old "good blogging," there are a few techniques that you can use to get other bloggers to link to you without resorting to crude tactics. These methods will attract more links while simultaneously making your blog more link-worthy:

- Post original opinions with a clear and unique point of view.

- Link to original sources whenever possible.
- Credit the blog that lead you to the source with a link.
- Blog with great frequency, daily is best.
- Use permalinks or post pages to make your entries more linkable.
- Link to other bloggers.
- It is okay to e-mail bloggers to let you know that you have linked to them, but do this sparingly.

Reciprocal Linking

The Internet is built on links; it's how it works, but you need not feel obligated to link back to a fellow blogger just because he or she has sent you some traffic. Feel free to do so if you wish, but if you do it out of obligation and you are constantly linking to anyone who links to you, your blog will suffer for it. Link to a blog that you enjoy or feel your readers might enjoy. Thinking through your linking means you are participating in the blogging community and making it stronger—but only if your links are genuine.

The Blogosphere-Friendly Link

Beyond the HTML mechanics of creating a hyperlink (discussed in Chapter 4) bloggers have developed a kind of creative linking method that serves a variety of purposes. In order to keep posts succinct, many bloggers will write a sentence that incorporates the link without breaking stride. Take a look at these two examples of a blog post that link to the Internet Movie Database for a particular film.

Post #1—a bland linking technique:
I saw *The Polar Express* today, what an awesome movie! <u>Check it, yo</u>.

Post #2—sophisticated linking technique:
<u>*The Polar Express*</u> is a great film.

The first post employs a weak, clumsy linking method that makes the entry clunky and longer than it needs to be. The second post is short and sweet: the link *is* the post, and it is brief and descriptive. Link-centric posts do not have to be pithy. Just think when you link. The descriptive aspect of the link is important in the blogosphere because blog-tracking sites aggregate the links that bloggers publish and display them by popularity. If you use descriptive words, your link alone is both a link and an opinion.

The figure on page 96 shows citations for a link at Popdex. Of the eight blogs shown, only one blogger used descriptive words in the link. Everyone else just used the title of the page: "Four-Color Hell." Thanks to the one blogger who used descriptive words, we know that "Four-Color Hell" is "a new comics blog."

Plum Crazy   10:22 A.M.
"Four-Color Hell"

Plum Crazy   6:39 A.M.
"Four-Color Hell"

undisturbed.org   4:48 A.M.
"Four-Color Hell"

The Johnny Bacardi Show   4:47 A.M.
"Four-Color Hell"

The Safety Valve   3:40 A.M.
"Four-Color Hell"

JUNE 24TH

Mother, May I Sleep   9:27 P.M.
   with Treacher?
"a new comics blog"

Solonor's Ink Well   8:48 P.M.
"Four-Color Hell"

Weblogs.Com: 5:24 P.M.
Recently Changed
Weblogs
"Four-Color Hell"

Could we just click on the link to find out what the site is? Yes. But following good blog link etiquette contributes to a smarter, faster, and more usable blogosphere while simultaneously streamlining your posts for punchier delivery. The owner of the blog "Mother, May I Sleep with Treacher?" knows this, and now so do you.

Blogging as Social Networking

In 1973, sociologist Dr. Mark Granovetter wrote an article called "The Strength of Weak Ties." In this article, Granovetter explained that a friend of a friend—somebody only loosely connected with your usual social group—is more likely to help you meet new people and land a job because he or she has a whole new set of friends who represent opportunities you've never explored. I think he even had pie charts backing him up. Very scientific, but it's not the seventies any more.

No doubt you've heard of at least one of the many social networking sites such as Friendster, Orkut, LinkedIn, Tribe, Ryze, ZeroDegrees, Ecademy, RealContacts, Ringo, MySpace, Yafro, EveryonesConnected, Friendzy, FriendSurfer, Tickle, Evite, Plaxo, Squiby, and WhizSpark to name a bunch. They're all based on the "It's not what you know, it's who you know" theory of getting ahead in life. There are so many of these sites that blogger Jason Kottke poked some fun at them all by posting a mock job opening on the popular want-ads site, Craigslist, for a Personal Social Network Coordinator. He listed the job as a "Permanent full-time position for a New York–based web designer." The specific duties listed included:

- approving or rejecting invitations of friendship
- managing a database of usernames and passwords for each of the social networking sites
- sending out friendship invitations
- keeping my social network synchronized; that is, invite friends from one social networking site to be friends in all of the other social networking sites
- handling requests by friends to be introduced to another friend that they might not know
- keeping track of my current likes and dislikes and updating my personal information within each service accordingly
- writing testimonials for friends
- various "damage control" functions when rebuffed "non-friends" become upset due to non-acceptance of their offers of friendship
- continually browsing my friends' first and second degrees for potential new friends and business contacts
- participating on any of the sites' message boards on my behalf

  Future duties may include discouraging companies and individuals from starting new social networking sites so that additional staff won't be necessary in the future. Past employment as a bouncer, "heavy," or hired goon may be helpful in this regard.

Kottke added that telecommuting was permitted and there was a fringe benefit: addition as his friend in all of the sites he belongs to. The posting was intended to highlight the fact that these services are overwhelming to the standard user and ultimately flawed because they do not represent everyday life. They have been built from the top down by engineers who think they know what you need, and users are supposed to obey the rules rather than just adapt the parts that work for their own needs. The programmers who build these services need to understand how people really use software. When it comes to software, we're really just a bunch of primates being shown a new tool and we should be treated as such.

1. Present us with a simple new software tool.
2. Watch and understand how we adapt it to our needs.
3. Cater to that adaptation

Admittedly, social networking sites are fun, and there are lots of people who do find love, friends, and jobs by participating in them. Still, something seems to be missing. Once you've persuaded all your friends to join and you have a virtual network numbering in the hundreds of thousands, what are you supposed to get out of it? What if you already have enough friends and a job?

Before the clonesters started busting out all over, an accidental social network had already begun to grow strong on the web. This network was blind to height, weight, and eye color—a virtual world in which thoughts, opinions, and ideas represent the people who had them. This world was born, not built. Within it, people are drawn together by intellectual attraction; news and knowledge is prized over crushes and turnoffs. The blogging world started with the big bang of Blogger.com in 1999 and has been expanding ever since.

Publishing your thoughts, observations, opinions, or even just a collection of links to your blog speaks volumes about who you are, and it means so much more than "I want to date: women. My sense of humor is: raunchy." Incidentally, it's very funny to say that with an Arnold Schwarzenegger voice.

I'll be the first to admit that social networking sites in some evolved form are potentially invaluable to the future of our connected lives, but I'd also like to point out that blogging is and has been the ultimate networking tool for quite some time now. On Mother's Day of 2004 Blogger launched a feature in response to the usage patterns of users. For years, people had been putting a picture and a short biography in the sidebar of their blog and would often have an "about me" page for more information. Blogger Profiles catered to that practice and made it easier.

Blogrolling

Blogrolling—the practice of publishing a link list of blogs—is significant because it strengthens the blogging network and helps generate weak ties. Weak ties are very important in any social network. They play important roles in a number of activities from finding love to getting a job. A blogroll is a simple hyperlinked listing of blogs, usually in the sidebar of a blog.

XFN, the Xhtml Friends Network, is a simple way to represent human relationships within hyperlinks. Used together with blogrolling, XFN enables bloggers to indicate their relationship to the people in their blogrolls by adding a "rel" attribute to their <a href> tags. Example:

<a href="http://bizstone.com"rel="friend met">Biz</a>

Social networking applications popped up all over the place in 2003 and 2004. These are websites that allow users to add friends to a database and then explore pictures and profiles of people they are connected to through those friends. Blogrolling is similar to adding friends, but possibly more significant. When bloggers add a link to their blogroll, they are adding another blogger they may or may not know personally but are

PageRank is Google's method of determining the value of a web page. A link from page A to page B is considered a vote, by page A, for page B. Google also takes into consideration the value of the page casting the vote. So, when a high-ranking blogger links to you, they are not only sending you traffic but also sharing some wealth.

intellectually attracted to. This makes for a far more thoughtful "intellectual ecosystem" that has applications beyond those of a dating service.

Blogrolling is an adopted practice, but it is also the name of a website created by Jason DeFillippo. Blogrolling.com makes it easy for people to create and maintain a list of favorite bloggers. These blogrolls express connections between blogs. When you have a blogroll on your blog you are saying, "These are my favorite blogs; I recommend them." Furthermore, you are telling the bloggers in your list that you like them and that they may very well like the blogs they are listed with. You are defining your community and telling others that you see yourself as the company you keep.

Blogrolling services make it super-easy to add a site to your blogroll. To get started, you have to sign up to the site and get some code to insert in your blog template, but after that, adding new blogs is a piece of cake. All you have to do is visit a blog you like, and two clicks after that, you've added it to your blogroll. Except for the initial setup, which is just copying and pasting, there's no HTML or template stuff to worry about.

Since the blogosphere is reciprocal, having a blogroll can help you get more exposure and enables you to become a more active node in the blogging network. When you link to another blogger, there's a good chance he'll spot you in his referral logs, and after reading your blog, might link you back if he likes what he sees. The more links you've got pointing toward your blog, the more potential you have to gain readership and the higher your PageRank climbs. So by simply adding links to your favorite bloggers, you may end up with more traffic, a larger audience, and more influence in the blogosphere.

If you're less of a social blogger and more of a topic-focused or niche blogger, these same techniques still hold true. Blogrolling other blogs in your niche will have the same effect or better as adding favorite blogs to a link list. Yes, you may lose a reader because they click on your blogroll and go to another blog, but you might gain a few readers from someone else's blogroll. Over time, plugging into the community of bloggers helps more than it hurts.

The Basics of Comments

Another way to embrace community is to spark discussion right there on your blog. Many bloggers choose to incorporate a commenting system into their blog. Comments are a way for readers to attach their two cents to a particular blog entry. When a commenting system is in place and enabled, visitors are provided an open invitation to type a comment and a button with which to publish it straight to your blog, thus adding their voice to yours. Commenting systems usually allow the author to decide if comments are wanted on a per-post basis. This allows you to decide if you want to invite discussion on a post before you publish it.

In an ideal situation, reader comments are an extension of the original post—a conversation that takes place right on your site and ads value to your initial thought. However, occasionally you may get a distasteful comment from a less than exemplary participant. Do you delete the comment or leave it? It can be a difficult decision to make because on the one hand the comment might annoy you, and on the other hand you feel that you have an obligation as the provider of this forum to allow a certain level of free speech.

If you have a comment that you are not sure about, ask yourself if the comment could be offensive to your core audience of readers and, even more important, is it offensive to you? This is your blog—an extension of you online—and if you are uncomfortable hosting this comment, then you should remove it. Deleting a reader's comment from your blog is about as insulting as blocking someone from being able to instant message you and it is possible to alienate a reader. You gotta do what you gotta do. More popular blogs face the threat of comment spam—undesirable comments placed on a site to increase visibility of another site. As with e-mail spam, this is an ongoing battle for which there are an emerging set of weapons and a plan of attack.

Who Owns the Comments?

Textbook example: Blogger Jason Kottke once asked the question "Who owns the conversation on my website?" when the number of comments on one of his posts exploded to over 700 in two weeks' time and continued to grow. Some web-hosting services will charge extra when a site exceeds its monthly data transfer allowance. This can amount to hundreds of dollars in fees. The volume of traffic caused an unexpected financial strain.

Surging bandwidth costs dictated that Jason turn off the commenting, but he was torn because the conversation seemed genuine and intelligent. He even compared the comments to a kind of group-authored series of books:

> Those 700 comments comprise a total of ~125,000 words (~180 per entry); that's about 3.3 150-page books ... Who am I to shut down a conversation that I'm not involved in? This may be my site, but the participants own the conversation. As much as it makes sense to shut it down, I'm inclined to let the participants go as long as they want. —Jason Kottke

Jason is a celebrated blogger with a true respect for words on the web. He ended up letting the conversation

Blogger Jen Garrett on Kottke's comment question: "Of course he owns the conversation. They left it for him on his site and now it's his responsibility. It's like when someone leaves a baby on your doorstep. It's yours now. Happy fucking Mother's Day."

find a natural stopping point and then found a less expensive way to archive the comments for public viewing. It doesn't really matter whether or not Jason owns the comments; he is responsible for them either way.

Managing Reader Comments

You will find that on some posts you do not want feedback from the peanut gallery. You simply have something to say and that's that. No lip. On posts that do enable commenting you will sometimes get punks posting unsavory remarks. What should you do? Here are some general guidelines.

- Take It Outside: Don't get into a nasty argument on your blog. That's like inviting people over to dinner and yelling at your spouse in front of them. The proper way to deal with a corrupt comment is to delete it and in its place put "Comment removed: off topic." Or something equally antiseptic. If you must get into a fight, take it outside—do it over e-mail.
- It's Your House: It's your blog; you own it, and you are in charge of the content. Remember, your blog is a web proxy for you; if there is a comment on your page that you feel uncomfortable publishing under your

name, you should go ahead and remove it. It's your house, dammit. You can tell them to get out of your kitchen. (Yes, it's clear that you are not the author of the comments, but note that search engines don't know that. So if someone leaves a comment about "how to commit murder," your blog may turn up when some freak searches for that phrase.)

- Beware the Backlash: Be prepared for the possibility of a backlash if you do delete or edit someone's comment. Some people may feel maligned or singled out if you remove their words. A comment code (below) can help in this situation.

- Comment Code: You may be able to avoid ugly situations altogether and stave off unwanted comments by attaching a note viewable to anyone interested in leaving a comment. Something along the lines of: "Robust debate and even unusual opinions are encouraged, but please stay on-topic and be respectful. Out-and-out nastiness will be deleted."

Leaving Comments

If you have the responsibility of managing readers' comments, then you should know how to behave when it comes to leaving comments yourself. Sometimes we forget. Be civil, make the point you want to make, but remember you are in someone else's house. If you want people to respect your point of view, be thoughtful, and proofread your comment.

**Read your comment out loud to see how it will
sound in other people's heads.**

Final Comments About Comments

Commenting systems are built in to all the major blogging applications these days, so commenting becomes something every blogger has to think about at some point. Comments are a great feature but also a responsibility. It makes sense to think about whether or not you are going to turn on comments for the content you are sharing with the world. It's possible to make a unilateral decision up front to always have comments or to never have comments, but you might want to think about being more selective.

Not every post is worthy of discussion, and sometimes you just don't need feedback. If you have the ability to enable commenting on a per-post basis, then it makes sense to be selective about when to invite a conversation. This thoughtful approach to enabling comments can have the added benefit of cutting down on comment spam, trollers, and flamers—nasty stuff.

Depending on the popularity of your blog and the nature of the particular post, it can be extra work managing your readers' conversations. If a post is incendiary and tips in the blogosphere, you could have a full-fledged blowout on your hands. Then you've gotta check in every hour or so and make sure there's no content on your site that you aren't comfortable hosting.

The flip side of the coin is that you could end up with no comments on most of your posts—which could harsh your ego buzz. You don't want that either. You also have to give thought to when it's the right time to cut the cord. Is a once-vibrant conversation now just a vegetable on life support? Is the conversation totally off topic and annoying? Are there a bunch of posts with links to buy some v1@gra? Then it's time to go in and close those comments. The conversation is over. Stop living in the past and go post something brand new and revolutionary.

Your Blogging Process

For some bloggers, it's enough to just write what's on their minds and be done with it. However, others look to the blogosphere for inspiration, feedback, information, education, and interaction. They need to wade around in the information muck for a while before they jump in and say their piece. To this end, many bloggers have evolved a kind of blogging process. You too will find a structure that works, something you will follow loosely in order to keep your blog alive and well.

Depending on your approach, blogging can be work. Some bloggers budget an hour or more a day for reading blogs, an hour for writing, thirty minutes on promotion and stat checking, and maybe an hour or so per week on community-related aspects of blogging like installing a blogroll. Sneaky bloggers will go out of their way to publish during "blogging prime time" (presumably daytime work hours) so their posts will show up on recently updated lists and blogrolls while people are doing their blog reading from their cushy, high-bandwidth connections at the office.

The benefits of blogging—such as increased writing proficiency and an increased ability to think critically— are enough to keep some people happily blogging away day after day. Others get burned out, mostly because they are not getting a warm, fuzzy sense of community and feedback. To avoid burnout and to build relationships online, employ commenting, check your stats, and publicize other methods readers can use to contact you, such as IM and e-mail.

In the absense of interactive elements, the blogging experience can feel like a lonely, one-way communication medium. One of the beauties of the blogging world is that you aren't tethered to a time-based conversation; you can compose your thoughts and come back later to read the comments. Even without interactive elements baked into your blog, sites like Technorati are finding conversations in the blogosphere for you. Just enter your blog address in a field and click a button, then read the reactions to your blog.

Some bloggers prefer a one-way approach to blogging. They are not interested in gauging community reaction to their ideas. If you have something to say to them, compose a traditional letter to the editor, e-mail them, and perhaps it will be read. But most bloggers have jumped into—and stayed in—the fray because they seek to build a relationship with their readers. They want to engage in conversation and build community around themselves and their ideas. This is why features like commenting and sites like Technorati have sprung up and become popular. It's why blogging has captivated the imagination of millions, and it's why the Internet is alive again.

Keep It Clean

Once you sign up and publish your first post, you have become part of a new media frontier. Your voice has been added to the character of the blogosphere. For an unexplored territory, it's pretty forgiving, and you're allowed to make mistakes—just avoid making enemies.

Blogging can be a cathartic exercise, a business-related enterprise, a group endeavor, or a one-person web newspaper. No matter what kind of blog you publish, try to maintain civility and strive for a modicum of ethical intellectualism. If a blog is the online version of you, then the blogosphere is the online version of our world, our home. As Olympia Dukakis reminds us, "Don't shit where you eat."

3

Why Would Anyone Want to Blog?

Without my blog, I'd be just another forgotten former child actor, dug up every decade or so on a "Where are they now?" program. I'd be frustrated and broke. However, by writing in my blog, I found a passion for storytelling, and maybe even a second career. I'm happy and able to support my family doing something that I love. —Wil Wheaton

My sister lives in a small house with two grey-hounds, three cats, and her husband. She makes great vegan banana bread. When I visit, the dogs get nervous. They take turns staring at me.

They keep watch just to make sure I don't unfurl my hidden wings and fly off with one of the cats.

During one of these occasional visits I will enjoy banana bread while chatting with Mandy (that's my sister) and Garo (that's her husband). I've already converted Garo to the way of blogging—he keeps a blog for his band. We will start talking about how Mandy would love to one day work for herself, maybe something having to do with herbs. She loves herbal remedies and knows a lot about them. Before long, the conversation inevitably turns toward blogs. It's a sickness with me.

"Mandy, you should start a blog."

Her nose wrinkles, and she says she could never do that. She doesn't like the idea of strangers reading what she does or knowing anything about her. Never mind strangers, she adds. Even worse than that, people she *knows* could go on the web and read about her. This is typical of someone who "doesn't get" blogging.

Don't misunderstand me, privacy is a valid concern in the blogosphere. What my sister is missing about blogs is that they are whatever you make of them. Mandy doesn't have to put anything personal on her blog. It can be more of a professional undertaking. This doesn't win her over. Her nose is still all bunched up, and now she's got one eye half closed. Some people need a little more encouragement. Or maybe it's just been a while since I last bathed.

If Mandy started a blog about herbology, she could

call it Herblog. Nice. That works on many levels. Okay, so Mandy is interested in eventually starting up a small home business somehow relating to herbs. A blog could help her in the endeavor. Let's look at how her herbal blogging initiative might play out.

She starts a blog with a simple editorial direction: surf the web for a few hours every week looking for herb websites, recipes, remedies, and products. Link to these sites and include opinions, reviews, and thoughts. If she allows commenting on her posts, her readers can help define her editorial vision with feedback.

She could kick-start her blog's traffic by telling all her friends and family about it. Or better yet, if she has some friends with blogs, she could ask them to link to it. She could also spend twenty bucks on grassroots text-based advertising, but she doesn't need to because if she keeps her editorial focus on herbology, Mandy's blog will start attracting web searchers and that's good because they're looking for information about herbs—and she's got it.

My sister could slowly hone her knowledge of herbs and homeopathy while simultaneously building a devoted readership. Let's say she keeps at this for one year. That is a year of knowledge retained in her blog, and, more important, her readership grows larger every month. With a good amount of traffic and a niche topic, Mandy could put some content-targeted advertising on her blog and make a modest amount of revenue. She's also well on her way to becoming the web guru of herbs. When people go searching for a savvy herbologist (maybe an acquiring editor?), they're going to land on Mandy's Herblog. Eventually Mandy will discover that there are several benefits of blogging. Some of these benefits are professional, others are personal.

Benefits of Blogging

It really doesn't matter if your blog is focused on a hobby, your work, politics, or just what you do during the course of your day. Blogging is information sharing, and the more you research and share, the more you gain expertise in your area of interest, even if that area is only "things that interest me." Every post you publish is added to your life's work, and that work is a window on your mind. Even if all you do is collect and publish bookmarks, the very links you choose to publish tip your hand. Blogging is an everyday practice of searching, thinking, and writing. There are many benefits to this exercise.

Blogging Makes You Smarter

With a seemingly infinite supply of information on the Internet, a blogger is forced to choose wisely when offering up a link. Then that blogger is tasked with adding succinct commentary to explain why that link is blogworthy. This in and of itself is not so hard, but

B logging makes me smarter because the people who read what I write are smarter than I am.

‑ Blogaritaville

doing it every day exercises the analytical mind because it forces us not only to choose what we think is interesting but also to pinpoint why we think it is. Then, we convey those thoughts in a short, descriptive paragraph.

Blogging is an information-saturated lifestyle filled with contemplation and expression. It doesn't seem like this at first, because bloggers are never expected to do much more than blast out a few posts a day as the mood strikes, but the cumulative effect is smartening. Is that a word? See how I think about these things? You can tell I'm a blogger.

Blogging and the blogosphere is all about the cumulative effect. Millions of blogs are making the web smarter and thousands of posts are making you smarter. Not just smarter either, but more successful. Let me give you an example.

Blogging Scenario: Getting a Book Deal Via Blog

I mentioned that an acquiring editor might spot Mandy's blog. This is not out of the realm of possibility. Back in the day, book deals were few and far between. You had to be a literary genius, a member of the super-elite writerly crowd, or some kind of insanely talented professional in your field. Then you needed an agent, a publicist, and a body of work to prove you had what it takes to be part of the chosen few, the noble, the proud, the published.

Now, you just need a blog and some chutzpah. Blogging is hooking people up with book deals willy-nilly. If you've always wanted to see your name on the shelf at Barnes & Noble and have an urge to tell your friends, "I can't come out tonight; my editor is breathing down my neck," then blogging is the place to start. There are bloggers out there on the web getting book deals right now. What are the secrets of blog-to-book success?

Become Obsessed

That's how I got my first deal. I became obsessed with blogging five years ago when I discovered how easy it was and realized that a revolution was at hand. I talked about blogging so much that my friends thought I was a freak, and people mostly rolled their eyes whenever I opened my mouth. But hey, I'm an author now. This obsessive fixation can work for you too. Obsessive behavior is treatable, but if left unchecked, it can land you some sweet gigs.

Julie Powell managed to swing her abnormal behavior into a book deal too. Down on her luck in Queens, New York, Julie said "Fuck this!" (I think she really did say that, she swears a lot) and decided to blog-u-ment her crazy scheme to cook her way through every single recipe in the 1961 first edition of *Mastering the Art of French Cooking* by the legendary Julia Child and Simone Beck—in one year. The Julie/Julia project was born. Five-hundred and thirty-six recipes in 365 days. "One girl and a crappy outer borough kitchen. Risking her marriage, her job, and her cats' well-being." Well, this "Government drone by day, renegade foodie by night" struck a chord with a prestigious publishing house.

People who become consumed by details are natural bloggers. Not just because they are more likely to blog every day and sometimes multiple times per day but also because they like to tweak, change, edit, redesign, add, remove, and fiddle around with their archives, profile, settings, template, etc. So if you are captivated by something and you have an urge to share it with people, now's a good time to start a blog. You'll thank me later when you sign that book deal. Maybe something along the lines of: "This book is dedicated to Biz."

Be the Blog

Salam Pax blogged from Iraq with bombs exploding all around him. The whole thing with the bombing and the fighting and the explosions is not always a good way to go, but in this case it worked out for Salam. It turns out people wanted to hear what was really going on over there and not just watch television news about how great America is. Actually, Salam got a sweet deal because his book is a republished version of his blog. If you can swing that, you're golden, because you've already done most of the work. Damn. I should have thought of that.

If you find yourself in a war-torn, bombed-out locale with just the clothes on your back and you feel you must blog, fret not. You can set things up so that you can blog with just an e-mail account or a cell phone. With audioblogger, your voice is published as an MP3 file straight from a phone. But don't audioblog if you're hiding from enemy soldiers, because they may hear you and shoot you. A living blogger makes for a far better blog.

Don't think about getting a book deal, just blog. That's what Mimi Smartypants did, and she was just not punk rock enough to turn down a book deal with HarperCollins UK. "I feel very guilty about this book thing, because many incredibly worthy authors struggle and suffer to get their books published, and many more toil away at brilliant novels in obscurity. I go blah blah during my lunch hour on my happy little subdomain, writing something that is not a book, and out of the blue comes a publishing contract."

Mimi went the same route as Salam: her book is going to be her blog republished in print. People, I can't stress how sweet of a deal this is: your editor does the work and you collect the checks. But don't get all smartypants just yet, you still have to get crackin' on that blog.

Be Part of a Dream Team

Meg, Matt, and Paul are three very smart and blog-savvy individuals who work well together. The publisher who put out their book recognized that this trio had potential as a group and realized that their combined know-how would make for one highly informational tome. You know things, and your friends know things too. Combined, you know more things than any one of you alone. It only makes sense, right? A group blog is a great way to start accumulating that knowledge. All it takes is one person to start a blog and then invite others to join from within the settings interface—many bloggers make light work.

Blaze Your Own Path

Wil Wheaton is an actor-turned-blogger. First with his blog, and now with his books, Wheaton has found the wealth of spirit he was chasing every time he went on an audition. Wheaton secured a three-book deal, and just like Sinatra, he did it my way. I mean his way. You know what I mean. Instead of waiting around for publishers to come to him, Wheaton self-published *Dancing Barefoot*, his collection of "five short but true stories about life in the so-called space age," and used his blog to promote it. He shipped over three thousand copies out of his living room in five months to paying customers and this is no small feat. Here's an insider tip: Publishers like books that sell. Now he is a big-time writer with publicists and the whole deal. Go, Wil!

You Can't Win the Lottery If You
Don't Buy a Ticket

Blogging is easy, and it's not hard to incorporate it into your life. You don't have to disclose personal facts unless you want to. Go ahead and make stuff up. Embellish. Kick things up a notch. A year from now I'll be picking up your paperback best seller, *A Year of Lies*, for $12.95. Good work.

Financial rewards in the form of a book deal or other freelance writing are not out of the question if you stick with your blog. You can't win the lottery if you don't buy a ticket. Mandy can wrinkle her nose at me all she wants, but when she's signing books at a Barnes & Noble in downtown Boston because millions of people love her novels about a skeptical herbologist who solves crimes with her amazing knowledge of holistic forensics, she'll realize that I was correct. And I'll be able to borrow some money from her.

4

Geeking Out

STARTING A BLOG, PLAYING WITH HTML

Dude. It's so easy to start a blog. You don't even have to own a computer; you just need access to the web to start a blog. Of course you'll need regular access to the web if you want to keep blogging. Let me also state for the record that I am being very casual with the term *access to the web* because you can blog via e-mail, phone, Palm, or an actual computer. I primarily use my laptop to blog, but occasionally I also use my cell phone or an e-mail account. It's not necessary to own a computer—yet another reason why blogging is democratizing the Internet.

Once you get into blogging and stick with it for a while, you may find yourself wondering about feeds, web design basics, or where to go for cool sidebar stuff. Those extras may seem like too much if you're a new blogger, so if you want to skip this chapter for now, that's okay with me. Otherwise, let's dig in.

Kevin "The Homeless Guy" Barbieux sleeps in abandoned buildings or shelters and uses free library computers to publish his blog with the intent of demolishing the negative stereotype of homelessness.

Getting Started

There are many applications you can use to blog. They range in complexity and price. I always recommend Google's blogging service, Blogger, even before I started working for Google because it's easy, free, flexible, and it's got all the features you'll want. Any web access will do—your home computer, work computer, a friend, the library—to start an account at Blogger. Creating an account only takes a few minutes. If you don't believe me, here's a preview:

Create an Account
- Choose a user name—you'll use this to sign in for future visits.
- Enter a password—this must be at least six characters long.
- Retype password. Enter it again just to be sure.
- Accept Blogger's Terms of Service—indicate that you have read and understand Blogger's Terms of Service.

(Among other things, you assume responsibility for any threatening, libelous, obscene, harassing, or offensive material on your blog, so be nice.)

Name Your Blog
- Blog title—enter a title for your blog.
- Blog address (URL)—you and others will use this to read and link to your blog.

Choose a Template
- Choose a custom look for your blog. (You can make your own or change this later.)

Compose Your First Post
- Enter a title for your post.
- Just type something, or upload a picture from your computer and type something to go with it.
- Click "Publish Your Post."

Congratulations. You are now a blogger. Just do that last step over and over again until you are rich and famous, or until you're sick of it. Your blog posts will accumulate on one rolling page with the newest stuff at the top. Once the page has a certain number of posts (you can set this) they disappear from the front page and get "archived." Your archives are where all your old posts get saved. Archive pages usually look just like your blog, and you and your readers can browse them any time to see what was going on yesterday, last month, or years ago—*everything* gets saved.

Sidebar Stuff

One of the first pieces of blog real estate you'll want to develop is your sidebar. A sidebar is a column that runs vertically parallel to your blog entries. Sidebars help make your blog into your home page by providing space for a grab bag of other information. Many bloggers will put a short biography in their sidebar and a list of favorite links. The links are often for their own convenience—sites they check on a regular basis—but just by publishing them, a blogger will tip his hand and tell us a bit about himself.

Henry, Your Sidebar Is Showing

Who is this mysterious Mr. Yee? Even after only a few months of blogging, Henry Yee had mastered the art of the link list. Most of the links in his sidebar click

Henry's Link List

my purple monkey—*friend*

carte blanche pedicure—*friend*

grey marble—*friend*

shall we dansu—*friend*

rachel pink rides the bus—*friend*

bloggy mcblogster—*friend*

spooky bear—*friend*

biztopher—*friend*

pascuzzo—*friend*

storrings—*friend*

So-FEEE-aahh:)—*friend*

aint it cool news—*alternative news*

design observer—*graphic design*

all music guide—*music reviews*

rotten tomatoes—*movie reviews*

the smoking gun—*alternative news*

Henry's Link List,

continues

new york times—*main-*

stream news

google news—*aggregated*

news

through to blogs or websites belonging to friends. Reading those sites will give you an idea of what kind of crowd Henry runs with: to sum up, his friends go out a lot. The last seven links on his list are to graphic design, music review, film review, alternative news, mainstream news, and aggregated news sites. So just from his link list, we can guess that Henry is a graphic designer who likes to go out with his friends to concerts and movies and likes to know what's going on in the world.

I'll admit that I have inside information, but just from reading his blog and glancing at his sidebar you'd be able to tell that this particular Mr. Yee happens to be the art director at Picador, a publishing house in Manhattan. He designs book jackets—nice ones—and watch out ladies, because he's not married.

What Does "Feed" Mean?

Feeds have been around since the late 1990s, but blogs and an increasingly voracious information-addicted culture have made them very popular. If you read any kind of website that gets updated regularly—especially blogs—then you may often notice little buttons or links that say "RSS," which stands for "Really Simple Syndication." That button means the site you are reading outputs a feed.

A feed is a machine-readable version of a website that gets published simultaneously in the background. Software packages often called "newsreaders" can be made to look for these feeds and use them for search or format them into yet another way to read your favorite blogs. To a user, newsreaders seem just like e-mail; sometimes they are on the web like one called Kinja, and sometimes you download them and launch them on your desktop like one called Shrook. These newsreaders can get the latest information from sites that provide feeds and present it to you. The value of this is that you can stay updated on all your favorite news sites and blogs by simply checking your reader throughout the day instead of actually visiting every single web page—it's just like checking e-mail. Newsreaders have been called "TiVo for the Web" because it's the web, on your terms.

Atom is a unified web-publishing standard inspired in great part by RSS—an early form of syndication that attracted attention and enthusiasm for the way in which it allowed developers and users to share and communicate personal content. However, as RSS grew in popularity, developers and specialists realized this early system could not hold up under the stress of increasing demand. A cooperative effort was launched to create a next-generation web-publishing standard that would be vendor neutral, easily implemented, freely extensible, and thoroughly specified. Thus, Atom was created.

What About Moblogging?

I'm glad you asked. Moblogging is short for mobile blogging, and it refers to blogging with a mobile device, most commonly a cell phone. Even the most basic, older cell phones can be used to phone in an audio post when used together with Audioblogger—a service that allows voice posting directly to your blog. These days, most new cell phones feature some kind of web access, even if it's just e-mail or text messaging. These features can be used to send text entries to a blog.

Shake It Like a Polaroid Picture? No.

The hottest combination of cell phones and blogging is photography. Camera-enabled phones, or camphones, are becoming more and more common. Capture a picture with your cell phone and send it to your blog. More over Polaroid; moblogging is the new instant camera. Sending photos straight to the web from your camphone means you can share your photos instantly with anyone who knows your URL. It also means you never have to worry about how many photos you can store on your camera-enabled phone because you don't need to store them there; you store them on a web server and delete them from the phone as soon as you send them off.

Communities of mobloggers are popping up all over

the web and all over the world. Browsing the latest photos at popular moblogging site Buzznet will get you candid photographs posted by people from India, Iceland, China, and everywhere in between. The potential of this phenomenon is huge. When enough people begin moblogging, on-the-scene reporting will be changed forever. Think of moblogging as distributed broadcasting. Instead of a television studio packaging up some news and broadcasting it to people sitting at home, millions of cameras are distributed throughout the major cities of the world capturing and broadcasting anything that happens immediately to the webs accessible to millions of others all day and all night. When a powerful image such as the caskets of fallen soldiers being flown home or a prisoner of war being mistreated is transmitted, we instantly realize its meaning; it transcends any language barrier.

This kind of information sharing is known as peer-to-peer or P2P sharing. You may recall the hullabaloo that Napster caused with P2P music file sharing. Imagine the same situation but with a different commodity: instead of music, it's knowledge, critical information, or maybe just a celebrity sighting. The press and traditional media usually get special passes to events like the Oscars. Enter one moblogger, and suddenly pictures are being transmitted instantly to the web and carefully controlled access is devalued. Once a popular blogger links to them, everyone will be able to check out the photos seconds after they are taken, beating any "exclusive" content a major television studio goes to great pains to package for the evening news. Simple, instant broadcasting available to anyone who can afford a cell phone changes the paradigm of broadcast media and empowers us all in new and interesting ways.

The future of peer-to-peer file sharing is not music or movies—it's information. Getting web-enabled cell phones into developing nations and showing people how to use them as a broadcasting tool could be transformative. The self-organizing power of a hyperconnected population is frightening to regimes that are used to the illusion that they have control over the information that citizens receive. When knowledge can spread virally anywhere in the world, we will be getting somewhere. In fact, there are similiarities between the spread of information and the spread of disease; we'll get into that a bit later.

Free Money: Putting Ads on Your Blog

When you put advertising on your blog, you get free money every month. I love free money. If you look around, you'll find that there are a few different ways of advertising on your blog and that there are several different services that want to help you do it—so they can split the profits. Unless you are a big-time blogger with millions of page views a month, you most likely will not be able to negotiate directly with Nike for a fat blogvertising contract. So signing up with a service that wants to share the profits is the way to go—shared profits is better than no profit, right?

There's two stand-out blog advertising services. One is Google's AdSense and the other is BlogAds. You can also sign up to be an Amazon Associate and make a small commission on any sales generated through your referral, so I suppose there are three proven methods. The Amazon Associates program is a little different and it's chump change, but still, it is nice when you forget about it and a gift certificate for ten bucks shows up in your e-mail.

AdSense for Bloggers: BlogSense?

Here's the secret insider tip for putting AdSense Ads on your blog: don't put them on your blog—put them on your post pages. See, the ads are content sensitive; that means they are relevant to the text of the page they cohabitate. When you put them on your main blog page, which changes every day, they can get kind of schizophrenic, and then they're really no good to anyone. But if you set the ads up to display on your blog's post pages—the individual archive page of each post—then they will learn the content on that page and serve up highly relevant advertising. When visitors arrive at your post page from a search result or some other link, they may very well click on one of your ads and earn you some money. It won't be a lot of money, but it adds up over time, and you can sign in to your account to keep an eye on your earnings.

I posted something once about book-cover design. With AdSense on that post page, the page earns me a dollar a day. That's not a lot but think about this: I have published nearly two thousand posts since starting my blog. Sure, they're not all going to earn a dollar a day, but the idea that every post has the potential, once published, to just keep on earning a dollar a day—that's motivation.

How to Sign Up for AdSense

You have to sign up and be approved for the AdSense program so they can screen out hate groups, pornography, and other stuff like that. So you visit www.google .com/adsense, and you click a button that says "click here to apply." You just follow a few steps and wait for Google to e-mail you with approval. Once you're approved then you can sign in and get the HTML code to paste into your blog template. Now here's the secret geek tip for hacking your template so that the ads only show up on your post pages, where they will have greater impact: conditional tags.

Blogger's conditional tags allow you to specify which of the elements in your blog you want to show up on either the main page or the post page. Let me show you an example, and don't let the HTML freak you out because you'll just copy and paste it.

This is the code I copy from the AdSense website:

```
<script type = "text/javascript"><!--
google_ad_client = "pub-476238996995490";
google_ad_width = 728;
google_ad_height = 90;
google_ad_format = "728x90_as";
google_ad_channel = " "
//--></script>
<script type="text/javascript"

src = "http://pagead2.googlesyndication.com/
pagead/show_ads.js">
</script>
```

Then, when I want it to show up only on my post pages
I just wrap the Blogger conditional tag around it:

```
<ItemPage></ItemPage>
```

So it looks like this:

```
<ItemPage><script type = "text/javascript"
><!--
google_ad_client = "pub-476238986995490";
google_ad_width = 728;
google_ad_height = 90;
google_ad_format = "728x90_as";
```

```
google_ad_channel = "";
//--></script>
<script type = "text/javascript"
src = "http://pagead2.googlesyndication.com/
pagead/show_ads.js">
</script></ItemPage>
```

See? That's not so bad, is it? It's good to dig in and try this stuff, because you start to pick up certain bits of information here and there, and before you know it, you're not afraid of code anymore.

Once you've placed the ad code in your template, you can just leave it there and blog as you normally would. Or, if you're like my friend Simon, who says that making more money is a hobby, then you might be interested in maximizing your Adsense profits. Here are a few common practices that the BlogSense kiddies have picked up:

- Getting Accepted: The best way to make sure you are within the AdSense quality threshold is to make certain your blog is rich in information. Try to work essays and product reviews into your posts.
- Post Pages: Put the AdSense code on your individual post pages instead of your main blog. (I already told you that. Nice.) When people click one of the ads, they will leave your site, which is sad, but you will be making money, which is happy. Happy and sad. See how emotional AdSense can be?

- Tracking Your Progress: AdSense has tracking tools to help you find out which pages are generating the most clicks and which ones are making the most money per click. Check out that spread and double down.
- Content Is Still King: Become a content machine. Generate a steady flow of content, and your traffic will pick up along with your revenues. Good content increases the depth of your site and lines your pockets.
- Try Some New Positions: Look at your stats and figure out if the ads make more money if they are on top of your post, along the side underneath, wherever. Read the *Kama Sutra* if you have to. AdSense also offers different ad formats, from little ones to big ones to really big ones. Fat ones too. Try them all and find out which are best.
- Write Goodly: Don't *try to sell* but offer reviews of stuff when applicable: *Why* do you like your new digital camera? What model is it? Good writing, prolific posting habits, and paying attention to your stats will put you on the path to maximizing your monetization. How corporate I've become.

Signing Up for BlogAds

All the cool kids are doing it. Actually, scratch that, all the politically opinionated old men are doing it. Blogads.com is a small outfit founded by a man who is passionate about blogging—Henry Copland. The first time I met Henry was when he came to visit me while I was still working at Wellesley College. He had taken a special trip just to talk with anyone whom he considered to be a kindred blogger. He had just launched the new advertising website and was looking for feedback. Today, BlogAds are popular with the political bloggers such as Instapundit and Eschaton (atrios.blogspot.com) because they not only make money but tend to reflect the opinions of the bloggers who gladly deposit the checks. Unlike AdSense, with BlogAds, you may approve or deny the advertisers that want to run ads on your blog. In this manner, you have the opportunity to turn them into yet another way to express yourself while making some sweet side cash.

When you sign up at BlogAds you join "a network of influential bloggers who accept advertising." The advertisers order, manage, and renew the ads you have approved to run on your blog, and BlogAds does all the customer service. Here's the nitty-gritty on BlogAds:

- The average blogger makes $50/month.
- The big-dogs make upward of $1500/month.
- BlogAds takes a 20 percent cut of the profit.
- You customize your BlogAds selling page.
- Installation is cut-and-paste (like AdSense).

Basically, BlogAds is as easy or easier than AdSense, and it gives you more personal expression power—which is big with blogs. Of course, you can also do both, but you've got to keep in mind how it might junk things up. If you were to install both advertising systems you could put BlogAds on the main blog page and AdSense on the post pages. That would work because BlogAds is not content sensitive. Then you'd have the best of both worlds.

Going for the Trifecta: Amazon Associates

Amazon Associates is best used subtly throughout your blog. When you sign up for the associates program (associates.amazon.com), you have the option of placing all sorts of banners and boxes and whatnot on your website or blog, but the bloggers in the know realize that a link to any Amazon.com product page can be a moneymaker if you know how to insert your Associates ID into an Amazon product page URL. Xanga and TypePad bloggers who are also Amazon associates have the added advantage of automatic Associates ID insertion into any Amazon product page—the link to in a blog post—the software recognizes Amazon. Bloggers who hand-code their links or use another blogging provider will need to know where to place the code. Take a look below at how I've inserted my Associates ID into the Amazon Product page URL.

```
1.) http://www.amazon.com/exec/obidos/tg/
detail/-/0312330006/
```

```
2.) http://www.amazon.com/exec/obidos/tg/
detail/-/0312330006/specialcode
```

Now if I want to create a link to that page in a blog post, I would use the second URL as the destination instead of the first. They are identical except that the second one has "specialcode" right after the slash. They'll both work, but in order to earn a commission from any sales that may occur from a shopper heading over to Amazon from my blog I have to use Associates ID in the URL. That's how Amazon knows I sent them the business. You could make your blog and advertising trifecta if you put BlogAds on the main page, AdSense on the post pages, and Amazon Associates whenever you blog about a book, an album, or a power tool. However, I don't recommend doing this because when are you going to find time to blog? Pick one of these services and stick with it—remember, the better your blog is the more traffic it will attract, and the better your chances are of making more money. Advertising should come after content and general pride-in-ownership of your blog.

Blog Design Principles

Blogging software providers almost always offer professionally designed blog templates that meet most if not all web design standards, but many bloggers like to infuse their blog's design with a bit of their own personality.

Above all else, a well-designed blog is easy to read and easy to navigate. If you get your hands on a copy of Dreamweaver and feel like digging into your blog's design, try to keep these guidelines in mind.

Readability

Things to consider when attempting maximum readability are font size, colors, layout, cleanliness, and white space. White space is a term which refers to an area of a page where no elements are displayed and it's important because it allows the text to "breathe." Choose a light-colored background and dark text and don't skimp on the white space. If you keep those two things in mind, you will go a long way toward a clean, readable blog. Resist the temptation to make the font size tiny and the line height tight to "save space." The blank areas on a blog where text and illustrations are not printed is important. Don't be afraid of it. Blog designers should consider white space an important graphic element when working on a blog's layout.

Usability

Usability is a generic term that refers to design features that enable something to be user-friendly. The term, and the ideas it encompasses, can be applied to anything from a pen to a mall, but we're using it to refer to what makes a blog user-friendly. Okay? Good. Things to think about when striving for good usability in the blogging world are consistency in navigation, perma-links, easy access for reader feedback, prominent archives or search, and browser compliance.

If you have other features on your site—like an "About Me" page, a photo gallery, or an essay section—they are where a consistent navigation comes into play. You should put the links to these sections in the same place on every page of your site so your readers don't have to figure out where they are more than once. Permalinks or post pages are must-haves if you ever want other bloggers to link to you. And you do. A permalink or a post page just means that every one of your posts has some kind of per-manant address so readers can get right to it even months after it has disappeared from your blog's front page.

You can add a free site search as well as web search. Just copy and paste some code into your blog template, then replace the words "YOUR DOMAIN NAME," which appears three times in the code, with your own blog's actual domain name. Here's where you can get that code: http://www.google.com/searchcode.html.

You'll want prominent archives or a search mechanism for your blog because it adds value to your readers. One of the most desirable aspects of blogging is the fact that everything you post is archived and can be accessed days, months, or years later. I sometimes read my old archives just to remember what I was up to in, say, July 2001. (I was adopting my cat, Bruce, from an animal shelter in Los Angeles.) If you don't list your archives in the sidebar of your blog, you should at least have "search."

Browser compliance means that your blog template code is up to snuff according to the fine folks at the Web Standards Project (WaSP). Don't mess with them; they sting. If you want to make sure your blog is going to work with different browsers, you can ensure its compliance by visiting the Web Standards website (http://www.webstandards. org/). Run your URL through their validator and see if you need more work.

The Web Standards Project (WaSP) fights for standards that reduce the cost and complexity of development while increasing the accessibility and long-term viability of any site published on the web. They work with browser companies, software providers, and peers to deliver the true power of standards to the web.

HTML Hints for Blogging

HTML is one of the more frustrating things about blogging when you first get started. Blogging is no longer just for geeks, but no matter how WYSIWYG (what you see is what you get) your blogging software is, there will always be a little bit of HTML that you'll want to do. And you'll need to conquer your fear of HTML even if you plan to do simple stuff like paste in the code for AdSense or search. The best way to get into the world of

HTML is to learn a few basic tips and tricks that all the blogging geeks already seem to know. Here's a bunch of stuff that you'll use a lot in your blog posts.

How to Make a Hyperlink

1.)

`<a href= "http://www.bizstone.com">Biz Stone is a genius </a>.`

2.)

<u>Biz Stone is a genius</u>.

The first example above is the HTML that will render the second example above—a humble sentence that links to my blog. Notice that I did not hyperlink the period. I closed the tag just before it. Pretty sneaky, huh? HTML is a language, just like English. In fact, HTML stands for Hypertext Markup Language. There's no reason to be afraid of it. Look, I'm going to subtitle the perfectly pleasant conversation that the HTML is having with a web browser to prove it to you.

HTML: <a href="

ENGLISH: I'm about to give you a website.

HTML: http://www.bizstone.com

ENGLISH: This is the website I said I was going to give you.

HTML: ">

ENGLISH: Okay, I've given you the website, and now I'm going to give you the text I want people to be able to click on in order to get to that website.

HTML: Biz Stone is a genius
ENGLISH: Here's the text I want hyperlinked.

HTML: </a>
ENGLISH: Enough with the hyperlinking already.

HTML: .
ENGLISH: Here's some punctuation, punk.

Okay, that last part was uncalled for, but if the HTML is formatted correctly, then the web browser will pretty much just say "okay" to everything and render it properly. If the HTML is messed up, the browser might get confused and do weird stuff. But see? HTML is just a perfectly pleasant language. In fact, it's much more concise than English, don't you think? Here are some more HTML goodies you might want to use in your posts. Try typing some of this code into a blog post and click "Preview" to see the results—you're writing HTML. Woot!

How to Make a Horizontal Rule

```
<hr>
```

The *hr* stands for "horizontal rule." The code above will tell a web browser to insert a standard-issue horizontal rule wherever you put it.

```
<hr size=4>
```

Inserts a horizontal rule and sets a size (thickness) in pixels. In this case, four pixels thick. That's a nice, bold line.

```
<hr width=80%>
```

Inserts a horizontal rule and sets the width of the rule to a percentage relative to its surroundings, or if you leave off the percent sign, an absolute value in pixels.

```
<hr noshade>
```

Inserts a horizontal rule without the standard shadow effect.

So if you want a horizontal rule that is four pixels thick, 80 percent wide, and doesn't have a shadowy effect, then you would type:

```
<hr size=4 width=80% noshade>
```

How to Make an Ordered List (Numbers)

```
<ol></ol>
```

This is the tag you wrap around your whole list.

```
<li></li>
```

This is the tag you wrap around each item in the list. So type this:

```
<ol>
<li>Broccoli</li>
<li>Carrots</li>
<li>Potatoes</li>
</ol>
```

And this is what you'll get:

1. Broccoli
2. Carrots
3. Potatoes

How to Make an Unordered List (Bullets)

If you'd rather have bullets instead of numbers, then you need to switch from ordered list to unordered list. All you have to do is switch one letter. So type this:

```
<ul></ul>
<ul>
<li>Broccoli</li>
<li>Carrots</li>
<li>Potatoes</li>
</ul>
```

And behold:

- Broccoli
- Carrots
- Potatoes

So that's how you can make lists in your blog posts. Are we on a roll or what? You want some more? I'll give you some more.

Basic Type Formatting

How to Strike Through, Underline, Bold and Italicize, and Teletype

Sometimes you need a little formatting to help you make a point. A strike-through is often used in the blogosphere. Discussions can arise in the comments associated with a post. Sometimes the discussion turns up information that proves the original post wrong or corrects it in some way. In these situations, just changing the post would be weird because then the discussion following it would not make sense to new readers. So a blogger will use strike-through to cross out part of the post and add new text that clarifies it.

```
<strike></strike>
```

This is the strike-through tag. Just wrap it around the words you want to have a line through them. So this

```
Someone should invent <strike>wireless
elevators</strike> personal jet packs.
```

will look like this

```
Someone    should    invent    wireless    elevators
personal jet packs.
```

Here are a bunch of other text tags that you can just wrap around any text you want to apply the formatting to. It's easy to forget to put the tags before and after the text, and most of the time when something is amiss with HTML, it's because you forgot to close a tag. That's the first thing you should check when something doesn't look right on preview.

```
<h1></h1>
```

Heading one tags create the largest headline.

```
<h6></h6>
```

Heading six tags create the smallest headline. (Yes, you can also do two, three, four, and five.)

```
<b></b>
```

The bold tag makes text bold. **Damn it Jim.** I'm a doctor, not a bricklayer.

```
<i></i>
```

Wrap these babies around some book titles to italicize them. Nice.

```
<tt></tt>
```

This tag creates teletype, or typewriter-style text.

```
<blockquote></blockquote>
```

The block-quote tag will indent a chunk of text. It's useful for those times when you want to copy and paste some text from an article or e-mail into a blog post and call visual attention to the fact that it's quoted.

> **Geek Tip: You can use more than one tag at a time. If you really want to call visual attention to some quoted text, try using block quote and tele-**

**type on the same chuck of text.
Like so:**

```
<tt><blockquote>Your
text.</blockquote></tt>
```

Some slightly trickier tags let you adjust the size and color of text within your blog posts:

```
<font size=4>your text
</font>
```

Only 16 colors names are supported by the W3C HTML 4.0 standard (aqua, black, blue, fuchsia, gray, green, lime, maroon, navy, olive, purple, red, silver, teal, white, and yellow). Learn more about web colors at morecrayons.com.

This is how you would set the font size to four. You can specify number one through seven.

```
<font color=?>your text</font>
```

You can specify colors by their hexidecimal code, which you probably don't know off the top of your head, or you can specify colors by name.

How to Include an Image in a Post

Most blogging tools provide buttons for basic formatting like bold, italic, and underline, and most of them also provide an image upload or file upload button that helps you post images to your blog. However, in the event that your tool of choice does not support image

If you use a Mac, you can find the URL of an image by holding down the **ctrl** key and clicking on the image. Choose "Open image in new window" and copy the address from the browser's URL field. On a PC, right click and get the URL from Properties.

uploading—or if it does, but you want to go back in and edit the image post—let me show you how images in posts work.

This is the basic code you use to use to insert an image that is already uploaded to the web:

```
<img src="name">
```

You replace the word *name* with the actual URL of the image, so it could look something like this:

```
<img src="http://www.example
.com/mypicture.jpg">
```

If you want, you can also align the image left, right, center, bottom, top, or middle:

```
<img src="name" align="right">
```

I like to use align ="right" so my text flows along the left side and continues underneath the photo—a technique that works well with smaller images.

Geek Tip: You can force an image to display smaller in your post by adding width=100.

Here's how one of my image posts would look if I wanted to align the image right and force it to display in a small, thumbnail size:

```
<img src="http://www.example.com/mypicture
.jpg" align=right width=100>
```

A Touch of Style

Style sheets, when attached to documents, describe how the document should be displayed or printed. A CSS document is attached or embedded into the HTML code to influence its layout when accessed via a browser. CSS supports cascading, which means a single document may use two or more style sheets that are then applied according to specified priorities. Here's a bit of style that I have in one of my blog's templates:

```
<style type="text/css">
p {
    padding-right: 10px;
    padding-left: 10px;
    padding-top: 0px;
    font-family: Georgia
    font-size: small;
    line-height: 19px;
}
</style>
```

I know it looks scary, but CSS, or cascading style sheets, is the way the web is going. Except for that first part with the brackets and stuff, you can see that things pretty much make sense. The lowercase "p" means paragraph. If I stick this bit of code inside the <head></head> of my blog's template, then anything wrapped in <p></p> tags will have the padding, font, size, and line height that I have specified. And since all of my text is wrapped in those <p></p> tags, it will look they way I want it to.

If you choose one of the professionally designed blog templates offered by your blogging provider, then you don't have to fiddle around with this code. However, now that you know a little about it, you might want to experiment. For example, you could go into your template and change the font from Georgia to Verdana and then preview to see how you like it. Wow, now you're learning CSS. Look at you. Unstoppable.

Belly Up to Your Sidebar

Here are a few popular sidebar features many seasoned bloggers like to add.

Photo Stripping

You can use a picture-sharing site like Buzznet to add a strip of your latest mobile-phone photographs to your blog. However, since Buzznet works by e-mailing photos, you don't have to have a mobile camera phone; you can use your standard digital camera and an e-mail account. Once you get the pictures from your camera onto your computer, just e-mail them to your Buzznet account. Camera phone users can send the photo straight to the site. If you have included Buzznet code in your blog's template, then your photo strip will update automatically.

If you are using Blogger, always save your template before fiddling around with it. An easy way to save the template is to copy and paste it into a text document and save it on your computer's hard drive.

Blogrolling

Already discussed in great detail for its social networking applications, blogrolling is a very popular sidebar feature among bloggers. Easy to set up too. Just visit the site, blogrolling.com, sign up, and then click "Get code." Paste the code in your blog's template where you want your blogroll to show up. Of course, nothing will show up until you start adding favorite bloggers. You can do that at the blogrolling site, or you can install the Blogroll It! bookmarklet in your browser's link bar. The bookmarklet allows you to make any blog you are visiting a favorite blog on the fly—they call it one-click blogrolling. Your sidebar will automatically update.

Sitemeter

Many blogging providers come with a stats-reporting feature. Also, some bloggers prefer to have an additional statistics counter because they have found a service whose reporting they particularly like. I've used the free Site Meter (sitemeter.com) service for many years. I mostly just pay attention to the links that tell me who is linking to my blog—I like to visit them and see what they have said about me. (It's not always nice, but I'll take what I can get.)

All Consuming

All Consuming is a website created by Erik Benson in his spare time. It watches blogs for books that bloggers are citing and displays the most popular ones on an hourly basis. You can use the site to add a list of books to your blog's sidebar; all you have to do is copy and paste a little code into your blog's template. Maintain a list of what book or books you are currently reading and display it in your sidebar. Like the photo strip and the blogroll, the books you read tell readers more about you than loads of extra verbiage would.

You Are Your Blog

The artifacts you include in your sidebar, the font you pick for your posts, and the description you write in your blog settings are all extensions of your virtual self. People read and publish blogs because they recognize that there is a way to put themselves into this virtual world and interact within it. With every new sign-up to Blogger, our world gets a little smaller—and the web gets more character.

5

Blogging in Business

In 2003 a few innovative companies were launching blogging initiatives, and by 2004 many smaller businesses, entrepreneurs, and even large corporations started realizing that blogging is where it's at. Blogging is a savvy way to share knowledge and experience not just among employees but also with customers and potential new markets. Blogs are a cheap return on investment for any business.

Instead of deluging in-boxes with e-mail, clogging up the shredder with discarded memos, or dropping twenty grand on some dreaded knowledge management system for "enterprise class corporate environments," businesses can install a blogging application behind the firewall for a couple hundred bucks or point employees to a free blogging provider and encourage them to do their thing.

Why Businesses Are Using Blogs

Businesses are using blogs because they are sick of sounding like a bunch of corporate buttheads. "We at Stodgington, Drymann, and Heindlick value your personal initiatives toward the human attainment of financial enlightenment and at the end of the day, we want to be your trusted, trustworthy, trust-fund partner in life and beyond." Holy corporate-speak, Batman! Somebody get them a blog.

In *The Cluetrain Manifesto*, it is posited that giant soulless corporations churning out sterilized marketing-speak should soon be a thing of the past. Corporate mumbo jumbo is being replaced by human voices, voices of people who go home to families just like we do, who hate it when idiots run into their heels with shopping carts at the supermarket, who have interests, opinions, and goals. How are these voices getting out? How do real opinions and attitudes escape the corporate labyrinth and still manage to build recognition and gain influence in industry? Through blogging, obviously.

Internal Business Blogging

.Blogs have brought life to the web. People have discovered that there is an easy way to have their say. Everyone gets a voice, and the strongest voices are not measured by how loud they are; power in the blogosphere comes from the democratic process of other bloggers linking to good content. The best blogs bubble to the top. Voices that might ordinarily not get air time can command huge audiences.

The same phenomenon can be repeated in a corporate environment. You don't need to be a vice president to be heard. You don't need to worry that Phil from marketing will steal your idea; it's archived by date on your blog. Blogs have many uses in a corporate setting, because a big company is really just a mini blogosphere waiting to happen.

Blogger in Google: A B.I.G. Idea

Blogger was acquired by Google in February 2003. One of the first orders of business was to install a version of Blogger to be used behind the corporate firewall by Google employees. Blogger in Google was nicknamed B.I.G. The Google corporate Internet is one of the most amazingly vibrant and smart virtual playgrounds in the world; the installation of Blogger makes it even easier for Googlers to join the party.

Every company should have this. Hundreds of Googlers have their own blogs; many more participate in group blogs set up for a specific project. I especially love having a work-only blog because it means I can post all my ideas, and they're just floating out there for all the insanely smart engineers to find and very likely build within hours. Not only do I have a chronicle of my thoughts as they occur to me, but I have been collecting my work life experience since day one. If a "Noogler" wants to know what it's like just starting out, he or she needs only to read my archives from the beginning.

We also have a group blog called bHome that is open to those who work on Blogger at Google. This is a team blog used to keep track of industry news, competitors, potential partners, innovations, ideas, and projects. In addition to the main blog, we've got sidebar links to project proposals and outlines, keyword-based news alerts, and links to everyone's personal blogs. The team blog is set to automatically e-mail any new posts out to our team mailing list as well. That way if we're working from home or can't access the intranet for some reason, we can still be in the loop. We are literally on the same page at all times. When we talk at lunch we can just pick up where the blog post left off. It's like some kind of virtual version of telepathy.

Knowledge Management

"Knowledge management" sounds like one of those theoretical business-theory things that people talk about and then never do. In fact, it pretty much is. There are all kinds of "KM Solutions" available for businesses, but most people aren't going to log in to some complex system to enter their "knowledge"—whatever that means. If they do, it's because they're forced to, and half the time they probably just make stuff up.

Left to their own devices, people are just going to do what they know: e-mail, IM, the phone, and just talking over lunch. Blogging works with IM, phones, cameras, and any device that can do e-mail. In other words, it's everywhere and easy, and this accessibility makes it the system of choice in the real world. Plus, with blogging comes a certain ego boost that draws people back. When your words are in print and stats are being collected and discussions are being had all because of stuff you put out there, it's fun. You have fans.

People aren't likely to go back to their workstations to type up the day's conversations, ideas, phone calls, and e-mails. But this kind of stuff can be pasted or forwarded easily to a blog. Think of a blog as a database of experiential knowledge. Don't think of each little snippet of information as a work of genius; it's the collection of this stuff over time that's valuable. Copy and paste an IM conversation right into your blog. Call an audioblog entry in from your cell phone when you have an idea walking to the subway. It's like one of those "note-to-self" moments with an old-fashioned microcassette recorder, except this one is instantly published as an MP3 file on your blog. When you get an e-mail you want to share with others, just forward it to your blog using e-mail-to-blog features. And if you're one of those people who finds cool stuff on the web and then e-mails all your coworkers about it, then you're already a blogger. Just blog it. If your friends love getting this stuff from you, they can add you to their feed-reader (a way to stay on top of blog content without even surfing the web).

Businesses are using blogs internally to share knowledge, spread information through the whole company, and manage projects. Some of the ways that blogs are being used in business are:

- Ongoing notes from individual employees (when they go, the blog stays)
- Centralizing communication (instead of unmanageable disparate IMs and e-mails)
- Keeping written records of meetings, approvals, and ideas
- Building a single spot for projects, documentation, messaging

K-log is just a gussied-up name for a blog that is used in a more formal way. Blogging is easy and free, but if you're the person helping to set up blogs at your office, you've got to make it seem like a big deal by calling it knowledge management and referring to your blog as a "K-log." Seriously, it really is just spin. You can have a fun, easy, careless blog, or you can really pay attention and use it at work. I do both, and sometimes I mix it up a little. The point is, if you keep at it, your blog really does add up to something. Add to that a bunch of other employees doing the same thing, and you've got an active flow of knowledge and a constantly renewing idea exchange. Good stuff.

Businessfolks are taking their wireless laptops with them to high-priced conventions and blogging while the keynote is going on so the rest of their team back at the home base can read the notes. People are jotting down notes and observations about their job, the lunch in the cafeteria, their experience working with a Mac instead of a PC . . . whatever. A simple keyword search of your blog digs up your notes on a corporate presentation six months ago that somebody just e-mailed you about. In a world where more and more business is done via virtual meetings and digital correspondence, your blog is your secret memory weapon.

An internal, corporate blog should be thought of as a tool for an expert or employee to publish thoughts, insight, links to resources, important documents, updates on competitors, and other thinking so it can be archived, searchable, and browsable. Here's some stuff that a good

K-logger might have going on in addition to the standard features of a blog:

- A blog feed so readers can subscribe to the blog
- Mail-to-blog for easy publication of e-mails to the blog
- Comments to get discussions going on the blog

External Business Blogging

Blogging is your company's web presence on the cheap. Small Co. Inc. doesn't have the greenbacks to lay out for a designer, developer, and a pricey hosting package. When you start a blog, you get your company's name on the web, back it up with a real voice and expertise, and begin to own that niche on day one. Plus, updating a blog is cheaper and quicker than calling up your webmaster and asking them to code some changes and upload this, that, and the other. Just sign in and do it yourself. Update any time.

Blogging is especially useful for small-business owners, consultants, freelancers, and anyone who will benefit most from being known as an innovator in his or her particular field of expertise. Share your knowledge with a much larger audience, get your name out there. Be your brand and define your trade.

Blogging about related and timely content is a good way to bolster a brand. Stock art site Veer.com has a graphic-design blog called The Skinny; The Kicks Log is Kicksology's blog dedicated to basketball shoes; xBlog is expert thoughts on user experience and design; and it's all about the latest releases over at the Fox Searchlight Pictures' blog, which crosses over into the promotion realm. When the people behind the blog are genuinely into the subject matter, interest is generated on both sides of the screen.

It's easy to bend a blog toward promotion, but content still needs to rule. When Susan Orlean hired a blogger to build and write a blog about the film made out of her book *The Orchid Thief*, it was chockablock with real blog posts. When it comes to a good promotional blog, the blogger needs to be part actor, part writer, and part research lackey. The blogger needs to get something out of it—a little spotlight, a little ego boosting to keep them interested—but he or she also needs to dig up good stuff and publish it in readable, interesting posts that keep readers coming back for more. This can be achieved more easily if the blogger doesn't think blogging is work.

If they keep it up, bloggers can become self-made experts in their chosen area. Glen Reynolds gets hundreds of thousands of visitors a day to his political blog Instapundit; Matthew Haughey is the king of personal video recorders because of PVRblog; Martin Schwimmer is the go to guy over at The Trademark Blog; and if you're looking for a tax guru, um, there's the Tax Guru blog. Once your blog makes you into an expert, you have the option of branching out into freelance articles, books, seminars, etc. It's good to be the king.

Some of these blogs, like PVRblog, a digital video recorder group blog and Engadget a technology blog, are businesses in and of themselves, generating ad revenue in the thousands per month—plenty of money, especially when the blog is only a side job. PVRblog's creator, Matthew Haughey, is a creative director by day, and Engadget's author, Pete Rojas, is a freelance writer.

Blogs are often used as an easy way to update a press clippings page on a company website as well. A small start-up company based on one innovative product called Clip-n-Seal keeps track of press mentions, customer comments, and any other news on their simply designed website. They have a fresh, honest, open voice that makes you want to do your best to help them succeed—the kind of voice you just can't help but have when blogging. It's so cheap and easy, you don't feel the need to make everything sound super professional. Just drop some news and move on. Edit at will.

Software giant Macromedia jumped headfirst into blogging early on, launching a handful of blogs to be maintained by what they called community managers: experts on certain Macromedia products who could help spread information and advice in a friendly, nonsales way. It worked. Obviously, software companies are going to get into blogging as product service and support first, but more and more higher-ups in companies are beginning to realize that a human-powered machine-organized voice on the web beats a corporate "about" page any day.

The blog's not always the whole site, just the most lively piece of it. *Inc.* magazine's Fresh Inc. blog keeps the home page of the site up-to-date while the features pages are still published in traditional static way. This is a great way to merge blogging into an existing website. Just pick a spot and insert a blog. Fox Sports New England publishes the Bambino's Curse blog to cover Red Sox baseball in the summer and a Celtics basketball blog in the winter to keep their home page fresh and relevant. There should not be a magazine or news site on the web that doesn't have a blog; it's absurd not to give all those editors an outlet to do their thing. Not every story or fact is a feature, but even the smallest tidbit makes a great blog post and can keep readers coming back for more.

Blogs as Businesses: Making Money

Gizmodo is a blog that operates like a magazine in every way that counts except hemorrhaging money. It's part of nanopublishing mogul Nick Denton's Gawker Media Group, which publishes a number of blog-a-zines, including Fleshbot, Gawker, Defamer, and Wonkette, in addition to Gizmodo. Each blog editor or author is paid a monthly salary that on its own is probably not enough to live on, but these blogs are side gigs for the content creators. The blogs are specialized and get a good amount of traffic, so Denton is able to monetize them with advertising.

What about regular people who want to give blogging-for-dollars a shot? Matt Haughey's content sensitive success story is the one for them. Haughey was able to combine the one-two punch of text ads and a topic-focused blog. Haughey started the blog about personal video recorders like TiVo because he's a hobbyist and likes to tinker with them. He had no idea that he could make thousands of dollars a month just by pasting some ad code into his template, but he was pleasantly surprised when the checks started rolling in.

From his bio-page: Nick Denton has been involved in Internet media since 1996, first writing on the subject for the *Financial Times* of London and then founding two companies in the late 1990s. First Tuesday, an Internet-era events business with branches in 80 cities, was sold in 2000. Moreover Technologies, which is headquartered in London, provides news search technology to Fortune 500 companies and portals such as MSN.

How'd he do it? Haughey lucked into a magic combination: content-sensitive ads and a topical blog are like water for chocolate. First, let me explain about content-sensitive advertising. You may or may not know that

Google serves up keyword-based advertising along with search results. So if people search for "cars," then there are ads down the right side of the search-results page for—you guessed it—cars and car stuff. Google's Ad-Sense program (the program Haughey chose to use) enables people with websites to host the same kind of keyword-sensitive ads on their pages, and the ads will be based on the content of the pages. So if you have a web page about air conditioners, there will be ads for air conditioner–related goods wherever you decide to put them; Google provides the code to make them show up. When visitors to your web page click on any of those ads, your account swells. The rates can be anywhere from a few cents to several dollars per click.

It just so happens that TiVo and other personal video recorder (PVR) ads have a very high click-through rate. So instead of pennies per click, Haughey was making many dollars per click. You see, the ad buyers go to auction for those keywords, so when there's competition for the words, the prices go up, and that translates to more money for the people who serve the ads on websites. Matt Haughey's success was partly accidental because there were certain things he didn't realize that he later outlined for readers of his personal blog.

Haughey underestimated the popularity of DVR technology and he did not know that TiVo was a sought-after keyword. Haughey's other web projects, including his personal website, had high page rank and are featured prominently in Google search results. It was another happy discovery when he realized that by linking to this new blog from his personal site, Haughey was transferring a little of that search-engine gold and giving it some instant credentials—in other words, higher page rank. Haughey's sucess can be reduced to three key elements: focus, interest, and design.

Tips for Successful Content-Sensitive Advertising

1. A tight focus will earn more revenue with less traffic. Focus on something that can be purchased online.
2. Write a useful and interesting site. Don't just try to "turn a buck."
3. Design for search engines. Use pertinent page titles and descriptive file names.

Blogging is not the solution to every aspect of your business. It can be a small business in and of itself, but it's not a sure thing in that regard. A real tried-and-true advantage to blogging is that you position your brand and business on the web. Advertising revenue is icing on the cake.

Blogging beats traditional content management systems because blogs are thousands upon thousands of dollars cheaper than other ways to disseminate information, and they are easy. Most often, a business just wants an easy way to update some content, not a full-blown complex publishing system. Start with a free blogging solution for your business and spend your money on people. The most important part of blogging in business is a voice. In a corporate environment or as an external corporate message, blogging is about giving people the power to communicate when they need to in an organized, archived, and meaningful way. Blogs curb vacuous corporate speak and replace logos and meaningless mumbo jumbo with the power of a human voice.

BIZ STONE

6

Politics and Pupils

THE IMPACT OF BLOGGING ON SOCIETY

Warblogging

In the hours after the September 11 attacks on the United States, the web came alive. Anyone who runs a community website or service can show you the record-breaking spike in their server logs on that day and the days that followed. Blogs were no exception. In fact, people were using blogs to let friends and loved ones know they were okay. Bloggers in Manhattan were chronicling the sights and sounds of their city in the wake of these unbelievable events. Web surfers turned to these blogs to find out what was really going on, to be directed via well-chosen links to news stories with new information, to get a sense of perspective from a real person. From this burst of web activity, political blogging was born.

They were called warbloggers originally, but as time has gone on they evolved into the broader political realm. Since 9/11, the political blogosphere has been an expanding space filled with argument and camaraderie. Traditional journalists are blogging as are bloggers who've never before written for publication. Most of the blogs are labors of love, though some have managed to make money from their blogs through donations and advertising. Beyond the ability to generate revenue, the most heavily trafficked political bloggers have something even more powerful: influence.

Whether they are liberals, conservatives, libertarians, or anarchists, political bloggers all agree on the power of blogging. They are a community of outspoken political junkies who, even when they are disagreeing with other bloggers, still freely share the coin of the blogosphere: hyperlinks, links that users follow to jump from one blog to the next and that promote each blog even more. These bloggers are a strong community of individuals who realize they don't have the same influence as, say, the *New York Times*—yet.

But these political bloggers' power is even more impressive when you realize that they are influencing the influencers. Journalists look to the political blogosphere for fodder, commentary, quotes, and information. Given their track record and increasing readership, reporters must consider the political bloggerati when filing their stories—those facts better be checked or you might just have a Tennessee law professor pointing out your mistakes to his hundred thousand daily readers. Double check.

Who Are Political Bloggers?

Andrew Sullivan is an independent journalist for the *Sunday Times* of London and the former editor of the *New Republic,* a magazine he still writes for. His blog, Andrew Sullivan's Daily Dish, provides news and links to various controversial stories. His site, andrewsullivan.com, gets around sixty thousands visitors a day according to his public site meter.

Glen Reynolds is the web's Instapundit. His commentaries on politics, science, and culture are published daily to the world's most visited single-author blog—his. Visited avidly by about one hundred and twenty thousand people a day, Instapundit has more fans than most city dailies or cable news shows. If you have a modem, Reynolds has an opinion.

Markos Moulitsas Zuniga was born on September 11, 1971. His blog, Daily Kos, was born on May 26, 2002. Zuniga's liberal-leaning political blog receives over 2.5 million unique visits per month and he has turned his success into a venture—his consulting firm that specializes in the use of emergent technologies in political campaigns.

These men are the political protobloggers. They are the bloggers who spawn *blogchildren*—people who have been inspired to start a blog by reading someone else's. So not only do these popular political blogs enjoy vast numbers of readers, they also spawn more bloggers in their likeness who also grow an audience. In this way, the political blogosphere continues to expand and gain influence.

Blog for America: A Bubble of Community

Blog for America was the official blog of the Howard Dean for America presidential campaign. It started on March 15, 2003, and is considered the first-ever official blog of a presidential candidate. Dean's blog was updated and maintained by staff and guest writers as well as other contributors, but the real magic was in the comments feature.

On average, Dean's blog received about two thousand three hundred comments per day, and the campaign crew read all of them. When ideas, slogans, activities, and events were put into action from people's comments on the blog, Dean supporters knew that they had a very real part in the campaign. The blog had an infectious feeling of optimism; Dean supporters could join in on the campaign no matter where they were.

The Blog for America gave life to "deanspace"—a centralized bubble of support for the campaign. Dean's blog invented him. It put him on the map. In a world where journalists and reporters ask Google for their sound bites, Dean's blog and its supporters had them ready in the form of posts and comments. The blog was both a virtual meeting space and a machine for generating buzz and excitement.

That buzz and excitement might have hurt Dean at the same time it helped. The bubble of passion that grew around the blog was just that—a bubble. It's important to remember that while a blog is a strong tool for building a virtual community, it's still virtual. It's like when you run three miles a day on a treadmill all winter and on the first beautiful spring day you factor in that same half hour for a nice, outdoor jog—but it takes you an hour. There are hills, stoplights, curbs, and people in your way. It's the real world, and you're not in as good shape as you thought you were.

Deanspace was filled with Dean supporters. They whipped one another up into a frenzy. They lived in an echo chamber. Traditional media were attracted to this hub of online activity, and from that perspective it looked like Dean was way out in front, until the actual campaigning began and he started running into some of those hills and stoplights. It's key to remember that a blog and the community that surrounds it can open doors, but you can't rely on it entirely—unless you're running for virtual president.

The Blogging of the President

Dean kicked it off, and within months the blogging of the president 2004 was a given for the other campaigns. John Edwards, Wesley Clarke, Joe Lieberman, George Bush, and John Kerry all started rounding up their supporters on the web with presidential campaign blogs. If they didn't own some of the intellectual space in the blogosphere, the political bloggers would own it all and would have to speak for them on the web. In 2004, bloggers were credentialed at the democratic and republican conventions.

Democratic Journalism

In the 2004 presidential election, the boys on the bus were joined by the political bloggers. Standing on their software soapboxes, these laptop pundits planted the seeds of change. Their mission was to influence political journalism and maybe even democracy as we know it by taking control of the Internet and beaming their ideas into the minds of millions before big media had time to let the ink dry.

Unrestricted, unedited websites powered by passionate individuals can command the readership of a city daily and break important news gathered from e-mail tips and personal networks of sources. They're not all professionals; there's no editing going on; and usually there's not even a hint of objectivity. Still, these bloggers are reshaping political journalism and building a new force to be reckoned with.

Mainstream news media are forced to follow stories bloggers just won't let lie, like the scandal that ousted Senate Majority Leader Trent Lott, which Glen Reynolds and Josh Marshall refused to let die. Bloggers are a major development in the future of politics, taking the media out of corporate hands and giving them to the people. Two thousand four will be remembered as the year the Internet became a necessity for campaigning.

Blogging in Education

In the same way that political pundits and supporters are realizing that blogging is emergent democracy for the masses, teachers and students are getting hip to the learning potential blogs provide. The power to publish has always been on the wish lists of most teachers. The chalkboard at the front of the classroom gives that away. What's different about this new chalkboard is that the students can write on it too. From their seats. From their bedrooms. From any web connection anywhere in the world and at any time of day or night.

Traditionally, students in Professor Carlos Ramos's Culture and Civilization of Spain class at Wellesley College kept journals during the semester and passed them in at the end for a pass or fail grade. Only Ramos reads the journals, and he suspected a number of his students just wrote the whole thing the night before it was due. They weren't keeping a journal of all things relating to Spanish culture, which was the assignment. They weren't tracking current events or participating in the news and gossip of the day. Something had to be done.

In 2003 fellow blogger and associate editor of *Wellesley* magazine, Jennifer Garrett, and I helped Professor Ramos get what he wanted: blogging in the classroom. With a zero-dollar budget, no support from the college IT department, and by sneaking out of our assigned duties (I should have been preparing for a workshop and Jen should have been writing an article), Jen and I managed to set up a solution for Ramos's class. We wanted to build a cozy community of bloggers just for the class, complete with blogs for every student and one for the professor, with comments enabled on every blog post so that students could read and then discuss one another's journal entries about Spanish culture. We also installed blogrolls that not only displayed links to each student blog but also indicated which ones had been recently updated.

We used Blogger.com as our provider because it was free and we wanted the easiest possible solution for the students, most of whom were not familiar with blogging. We password-protected the group of about two dozen students so that their audience was restricted to those participating in the class. Professor Ramos thought it best not to allow the general web populace to read the students' journals. So we obliged. It seems that educators and institutions are still wary of the raw, unsupervised jungle of lawlessness that is the World Wide Web.

The students were able to sign in and update their blogs at any time, and Ramos was able to read the entries throughout the semester rather than just at the end. In addition, students were able to share ideas and comments with one another and surf around this mini blogosphere to get ideas for what to write about and for reaction to what they had already written. Having a vocal audience is a great way to find your own voice. To that end, Ramos upped the stakes a bit by making entries in the blog fifteen percent of the students' grade and requiring that they actively comment on one another's posts.

Blogging is not something that can be picked up by everyone instantly, as our experiment showed. A handful of the students loved the medium and took to it right away. For others it took longer or didn't happen at all, a snapshot of what I have found to be true of blogging as a whole. However, blogging is now considered to be a subject worth learning about, especially in the world of education. With major institutions like Harvard, Dartmouth, and Wellesley, as well as several high schools, middle schools, and even elementary schools realizing that there's something there, blogging is unavoidably headed into the trenches of learning.

Early adopters at the ground floor of education are beginning to explore blogging as a teaching and learning tool in educational environments around the world.

More and more teachers and students are captivated by the blog's advantage over a traditional website. With an interface as easy as web-based e-mail and a chronological structure that lends itself well to frequent updates, blogging eases the flow of information between teacher and student and back again. When feedback and interlinking begin to take place among the blogs, the opinions, ideas, and content becomes knitted together into a whole that is greater than the sum of its individual parts. That's when blogging really comes alive.

How Are Teachers Using Blogs?

Teachers use blogs in their professional practice to establish credibility and develop a public expert status. Many of the teachers blogging right now are simply blogging about blogs, but that will change as the practice becomes more widespread. Networking and personal knowledge sharing is helping educators move faster and accomplish more goals. Professor Ramos used his own blog for course announcements and assigned readings while other professors are finding that a simple ongoing list of annotated links is enough to hold the attention of students and colleagues and keep them in the know. Ultimately, an educational blog is a repository of notes and knowledge accumulated over the course of a semester or a year, fully searchable and available for years to come by both students who took the course and those who did not.

How Are Students Using Blogs?

In Ramos's class the students' assignment was to use the blog for reflective writing or journaling. Students who enter their notes and thoughts into a blog have a searchable database of those notes from any web connection. Teachers will work more and more with their connected students to allow the assignment, submission, and review process to go back and forth via blogs. Students are already sharing course-related resources with one another whenever they publish a public post.

The Students Are Producing Knowledge

Most schools do not provide enough access to primary sources and varied interpretations of complex historic and current events. Students are usually presented one point of view as bare fact. They are then expected to digest this information on their own and submit their understanding of the information in the old test-and-essay machine that is school. This process is stagnant. The students' contributions are offered up in calculated response to the class requirements and assignments. Isolation is another problem because the students do not benefit from any kind of peer reflection and feedback beyond the conversation or discussion that may or may not take place in class. Emergent ideas have nowhere to grow and students are discouraged from making their written thoughts public until they have been spell-checked, printed out, and handed in. This leaves no room for iteration and the development of new ideas in writing.

Inside the Classroom

Some students will take to blogging right away and others will take time to get used to writing every day and writing for an audience. Students who are already confident in their abilities will have no problems jumping right in, and other, less confident students will seek the ego-boosting aspect of blogging for encouragement. To smooth things out and promote blogging in the classroom, there are a few things teachers can do.

It is fairly obvious that blogging works best for everyone, including students, when there are topics to write about that capture the imagination and spark a passion. This is of course true in any classroom, regardless of blogs. The first order of business is to help the students find a passion, articulate it, and write about it in a learning environment. Initially suggesting topics to write about can be helpful, but the most successful tactic will be to just let the students do their own thing. If they can be encouraged to blog every day—on any subject—they will find their voice and discover a passion.

Students need to be bloggers, but they also need to be blog readers and interact with the other blogs. They need to leave comments and make links. Reading makes them better at writing and the feedback turns into a conversation. Getting feedback encourages more posting and helps students develop their voice. Reaction from an audience is a mirror that helps bloggers discover their strengths as well as weaknesses.

Any blogger who is going to stick with it for a significant amount of time needs to feel as though people are reading his or her blog to feel the presence of an audience. According to some educators, it's important to have a protected and safe-feeling environment surrounding any sort of web-based activity, but it's beneficial to have a healthy and diverse debate. That means publishing to the web at large. College-age students can handle some graffiti-like comments. For younger students, perhaps a group blog moderated by the teacher would provide the necessary shielding. In any case, a guided blog, one authored by the teacher that highlights exceptional posts and in other ways drives attention toward certain links and keeps the ball rolling is helpful. The idea is to get the fire started; to kickstart the network so that it works on its own. The students need to be able to teach one another. A lead blog helps to pull things together and serves as a model from which to draw inspiration.

There may be a place where blogging itself can be taught in schools. Just as learning Latin helps students with other languages, so learning the ways of blogging

Special adjustments can be made so that passwords and permissions create a gated blogging community, but this can stifle diversity.

can help them manage all the knowledge they accumulate during the school year and show them how to look to one another for feedback, support, and learning in a much more interactive, immersive situation.

Extending the Classroom

In some cases—such as higher education and distance learning—the closed-off mini-community idea may not be enough. The Dean campaign blog was an example of people spreading good ideas and creating relationships across a diverse society. These benefits can be mimicked in education. Some people talk about "social capital" as a new way to benefit from interconnection. We cannot enhance this social capital by sticking with our old one-on-one communication methods or by hanging around the same like-minded individuals day in and day out. Ideas need to be circulated to other networks and exposed to different ways of thinking. We need to peer into the minds of and collaborate with people who are new to us. Connecting to different social networks by putting blogs out on the web to be discovered opens up two-way and multi-way conversations with new cultures.

The best way to connect with these social worlds is through the network of "weak ties" affored by blogging. Blogs are readable by anyone and offer a loose, casual, network of ideas. The price of entry is low; the threshhold is welcoming. The strength of the new connecting grows across networks based on merit. Individual bloggers help filter out the useless ideas and in turn contribute to a kind of collective wisdom developed across the network as a whole. Different outlooks, once roped in, can then be further discussed within the smaller, gated communities of strong ties. They can be brought back into a single classroom and provide an intellectual feast.

7

Living in the Blogosphere

My life sits atop a foundation—an aggregate of personalities cemented together through hyperlinks—poured by invisible masons in a dimension that Freud might have called the collective conscious, an ecosystem of connectedness, a web within the web, another dimension of reality.

By publishing my thoughts, opinions, observations, and ideas over the years, a professional career has emerged from my blog and taken me to an interesting and unexpected place: San Francisco.

I had never met Molly Holzschlag before moving to San Francisco, nor had I ever spoken with her. We hadn't even chatted over IM, and yet it is because of her that I am sitting here in a coffee shop on the corner of Kansas and Sixteenth in Potrero Hill writing my second book about blogging and looking forward to going in to my fancy job at Google tomorrow morning. Molly lives in Arizona. I'm from Boston.

In August 2000 Molly was the executive editor of a webzine called *Web Review*. When she came across my blog and read my bio, she knew she had found the right person to write an article on this emerging grass-roots phenomenon, this new media culture called blogging. After reading through my archived blog entries and getting to know me—or at least getting to know my blogging persona—Molly e-mailed me with the subject line "Want to write an article?"

Working with Molly on that first article—my first paid writing gig ever—was such a great experience that I began pitching an article idea to her about once a month for the next year or so. At the height of late nineties web craze there was a robust audience of web professionals hungry for new ideas and projects and ready to spend money on servers, hosting, and other related goods and services. So an advertiser-supported web magazine filled with interesting how-to's from industry specialists was a good idea. When the utopian atmosphere surrounding the web evaporated, *Web Review* followed suit, and my gravy train of writing gigs derailed—but not before I had written a whole bunch of articles.

No more paid articles about blogging meant more

time for actual blogging, so I stepped up production at Genius Labs. When I say Genius Labs, you may think I am referring to a glamorous start-up. I just mean me. Genius Labs is my fictional company. I like to say Genius Labs because it sounds official. Of course, I was working as the creative director of Xanga, a web start-up, at this time as well so I could only post so much.

When I left the start-up, my blogging really picked up. Unemployment is the greatest thing that can happen to a blog. Posting frequency goes through the roof, and grocery shopping with a maxed-out credit card makes for great material—especially if you're a Bostonian who suddenly finds himself in Los Angeles riding a bus to the 99¢ Store for a 40-ounce Taiwanese beer.

Everything else may have gone to seed, but my blog was still going strong. And a good thing too because it saved me from ending up as an out-of-work power ranger (don't ask). I was at my wit's end, hopelessly checking my e-mail and actually considering the possibility of making cra2y m0ney onl1ne when a subject line jumped out at me: "Wanna write a book?"

Hell yes, I want to write a book! No, it wasn't Molly; it was Kate. Kate Small from New Riders Publishing. Kate had been following my blog, so she knew exactly what I was up to and that I had some time to write a book. Are you getting all this? Do you see the crazy opportunities my blog has laid at my feet?

Well, damned if I didn't go ahead and write a book

for Kate even though I never actually met her. (*Blogging: Genius Strategies for Instant Web Content* was published by New Riders in the fall of 2002 and it holds up even now. I highly recommend it.) I never met Kate. Still haven't. How weird is that? Very weird. And it only gets weirder. Two words: Evan Williams.

Recently, at a bar in San Francisco's Mission District, a friend of mine was visiting from Los Angeles and Evan met us and some others for drinks. My friend asked how Ev and I knew each other. The answer? Blogging, of course.

In 1999 Pyra Labs was a web start-up in San Francisco. The product, Pyra, was an online team management tool or "groupware." The company I was working for in Manhattan was testing this beta software, and my coworker was one of Pyra's most vocal customers, offering feedback and feature ideas on a regular basis. When Pyra founder Evan Williams and employee Paul Bausch launched the now legendary spin-off application they called Blogger, I thought I'd try it out.

I was hooked immediately and started posting like a maniac. In 1999, there weren't many blogs, so few in fact that Evan and Co. could check out new ones as they were being created. Ev found my blog and linked to me. He called me a "funny weblogging designer." When I realized that Ev was the creator of Blogger and founder of Pyra Labs, I bookmarked his site and have read it daily ever since.

My obsession with blogging found its way into my work at Xanga. The somewhat directionless start-up I was working with soon morphed into a weblog community. I insisted we emulate Pyra Labs. Now Ev didn't just think my posts were funny; he had a professional reason to follow my blog: our companies were competitors.

Ev put me in his blogroll, and I put him in mine. We were aware of what went on in each other's lives. We were linked even though we had never met, or spoken. The closest connection we had ever made was when I had emailed him some questions for a *Web Review* piece I was working on.

In February 2003, Google acquired Pyra Labs. I was no longer at Xanga. I had left the company in 2001 and after a brief stint in Los Angeles I had ended up working at Wellesley College in Massachusetts. Having never met Ev or even spoken to him on the phone, I sent him an e-mail with the subject line "Congratulations!" and half-jokingly, I also wrote "Let me know if you start hiring." A few months later I received an e-mail back with the subject "RE: Congratulations!"

Ev is a man of action. He pulled some strings, and before I could decide if I really wanted to leave Wellesley, I was agreeing to stock options at a pre-IPO Google. I still had to be approved by various executives and I had to talk to a whole bunch of people, but that all passed in a blur.

Just before I left for San Francisco, I closed my second blogging book deal—you're reading the fruit of it now—and all of a sudden I was back "behind the screen" of the blogging industry. No agent. No college diploma. Just my blog. I had created a version of myself online that reflected my true self and interests and a very real career grew from it.

Molly found my blog, and she hooked me up with writing gigs. Kate found my blog and, by extension, my articles, and handed me a publishing contract. Evan Williams, who had been reading my blog from the beginning, wound up in a position to hire me at the company that acquired his start-up. I finally met Ev—obviously—when I took the job and I met Molly a few months later at a conference in Austin, TX. Kate? Still haven't met Kate.

In the *Matrix* trilogy, the main character, Neo, played by Keanu Reeves, has realized that reality is not really reality but instead a simulated version of reality. With this knowledge, he is able to accomplish amazing things like dodge bullets and fly. In this alternate reality, Neo is a superhero. With my blog, I have created a proxy for myself online. This version of me has gotten two book deals and a dream job at one of the world's most innovative companies. In the real world, I am a state-college dropout. How did I do this? Welcome to this strange other dimension within which I have *Matrix*-like powers.

I propose a name for the intellectual cyber-
space we bloggers occupy: the Blogosphere.
—*William Quick, January 1, 2002*

What Is the Blogosphere?

Blogs are digital entities sprinkled throughout the vast-
ness of cyberspace, yet they create their own connectedness. The blogosphere is the network of blogs that lives
within the World Wide Web—a web within the web—
but it is more than documents and hyperlinks. Behind it
all are many individuals who combine to form an aggregated entity with its own force; it is a new media ecosystem with a complex social culture based on knowledge,
entertainment, and the sharing of ideas. In many ways,
the blogosphere is fulfilling the original promise of the
Internet: a vast, digital democracy of interconnected
minds. In addition, through methods of operation inher-
ent in the blogging culture, such as blogrolling, blogging
is a naturally occurring social network based on intellectual attraction.

Like Hollywood—Without the Fake Boobs

Because he has been in so many movies, Kevin Bacon can
be connected to any other actor by six degrees or fewer.
Bacon is connected to Tom Cruise by one degree because
they were both in *A Few Good Men*. Mike Myers was in

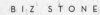

The Spy Who Shagged Me with Robert Wagner, who acted in *Wild Things* with Bacon, so Myers is two degrees away from Bacon. Even Charlie Chaplin is only three degrees from Bacon because he acted in *Monsieur Verdoux* with Barry Norton, who starred with Robert Wagner in *What Price Glory*.

A network is defined as "an interconnected system of things or people." The Kevin Bacon game is playable because the Hollywood system generates a densely interconnected group of actors linked to one another by the movies they've been in. Prolific film production and the mixing-up of these actors in a variety of casts makes the Hollywood system even more interconnected. This is how actors form a network. Likewise, blogs form a network. Replace the actors with bloggers and the movies with blogrolls, and you've got the blogosphere. It's like Hollywood—without the fake boobs. In fact, in the blogosphere we have our own version of Kevin Bacon whom I've mentioned before and who's name shows up in hundreds of blogrolls. His name is Jason Kottke. My blog is connected to Kottke's because he has the group blog Gothamist in his blogroll, and Gothamist has me in their blogroll. I am only two degrees away from Kottke in the blogosphere. Somebody pinch me.

It's a Small World After All

The links bloggers make to one another also mimic the social clustering that happens naturally all over the planet. There are about six billion people on planet Earth. Imagine a circle with six billion points on it. On average, it would take sixty million steps to travel halfway around the circle, even bounding fifty at a time. However, if you throw in a handful of random links across the circle, the average number of steps it would take to get from any one point to any other point becomes only six. The random links act like bridges connecting groups of people to other groups, dramatically reducing the average number of degrees of separation. Through these random links you can be connected to any other person on Earth in six links or fewer. And that's just with random links; we get a lot closer together when we get more specific.

These random links don't have a noticeable effect on our natural local clustering of friends and colleagues so they become somewhat invisible and cause us to say things like "Wow. What a small world!" when we discover that the stranger next to us on a bus in India works for our sister's neighbor back in Boston. What seems like a totally random link is the product of a weak tie between two seemingly disparate social clusters.

Weak Ties Give Us Strength

Mark Granoveter's article "The Strength of Weak Ties" is now famous. Granoveter explained that the links between people with whom we are not very closely connected are critical for spreading ideas or effecting change. In other words, all your friends may know you're out of work, but it's one friend's night-school professor who's more likely to help you get a job than all the rest of them put together.

To dig up new information you need weak ties. Strong ties are the densely clustered group of friends or colleagues you share your life with. A weak tie is the one person in that group that is also tied to another social cluster—a new, untapped reservoir of information and opportunity.

Say you have a good friend named Jason and you hang out with him on a regular basis. He knows you're looking for a job, but he doesn't know anything more than that. However, Jason's ambition to be a filmmaker drives him to take night classes in digital video editing, and he's struck up a working friendship with his professor. Jason is your weak tie to an untapped social cluster. At an end-of-semester party, Jason meets his professor's son, who is the CEO of a start-up media company that's looking for a full-time writer. Two weeks later, you have a job. Weak ties are strong.

Blogs as Weak-Tie Machines

Now instead of having a friend who goes to night school, imagine you have a blog—a frequently updated page that you pour your dreams, ideas, experiences, and expertise into. If they know about it, your real-world friends will probably check out your blog just to discover what you're thinking about, but there will be others. If you stick with your blog, you will develop a readership not only of your friends and family but of strangers too—people who return to your blog on a regular basis because you provide something that intrigues them or even outrages them. You will have an audience.

Through your blog, your thoughts and ideas have found their way into the minds of people across a bunch of new social circles. Maybe one of your readers is talking about what you posted right now at a dinner with friends. Did you post that you're looking for a new job? Maybe they'll recommend you to their boss at work. If they've been reading your blog for a long time, they may feel a connection with you. They may feel they know you well enough to at least mention your name.

Among your regular readers, there may also be fellow bloggers. Now we're really talking. If even one of these bloggers links to you or adds you to his blogroll, you are exposed to all of *his* readers, and you have just significantly enhanced your weak-tie quotient. Your chances of letting the world know you are looking for a job—or any other piece of information you hope will catch on and induce a physical, real-world reaction—have sig nificantly increased.

Blogs have a large amount of social influence, especially considering that the number of active bloggers is infinitesimal relative to the actual population of our planet. (There are several million blogs but not all of them are considered "active"—many are abandoned or not updated enough.) They have this influence because blogs help spread ideas and information across a network of weak ties. A single post in the blogosphere can effect real-world change. I can attest to the effectiveness of finding a job—my weak-tie machine hooked me up—but finding a job is just one example and a small one at that. When conditions are right, an idea can spread like a virus and the blogosphere can swarm into action, sometimes demonstrating an eerie group intelligence that seems to have a life of its own.

Rumors and misinformation can also spread through the blogosphere, but there seems to be a code among bloggers as a whole to sniff out lies and self-correct when things get out of hand. It may have something to do with what author James Surowiecki wrote in his book *The Wisdom of Crowds*. Surowiecki says a crowd becomes "wise" when it has a diversity of opinions from a decentralized group of independent members and a good method for aggregation. The blogosphere is a diverse collection of opinions published on independent blogs that are spread across the web and aggregated by search engines. So the blogosphere is a wise crowd and wisdom does not tolerate misinformation.

The Secret Zoo

In order to understand and fully appreciate the other-worldliness of the blogosphere, it helps to visit the concept of Traffic Zoology, first brought to my attention by Matthew Frederick Davis Hemming. I love this idea and use it as an example because it conjurs up the right kind of strangely inspiring scientific perspective that it takes to sense the existence of this other dimension of intelligence—a dimension into which we are headed. A kind of interdependent hyperconnected macro-organism that is unavoidably the future of our connected lives.

There is a secret zoo that runs encaged along the roads. They are liquid, semi-visible Goliaths that rage through the streams and chunks of ordinary traffic, with the effervescent tendrils of mile-long tails whipping behind them like Chinese dragons. Though composed of hundreds of pounds of steel, glass and plastic, they are able to pass through solid objects. They are bound by the laws of the highway, but not by any conventional notion of time or space.

They are aggregate traffic animals: A menagerie of emergent beasts drawn from the interacting behaviours of many individual human beings driving many individual cars with many individual goals, their collective activity giving rise to something with greater presence, power and purpose than the sum of its constituents. They take on a host of different forms, each to serve a different end. They are real, and they drive among us.

Hemming goes on to explain the different classifications of beasties he has noticed while studying the emergent behavior of traffic in Ontario, Canada. We are informed that the most basic type of Aggregate Traffic Animal (ATA) is the Asipetal Caterpillar, also known as a worm. These worms come into existence when a stable solo vehicle spawns a linear, single-lane chain of vehicles.

The second most common ATA is a more fleeting creature that manifests itself as a single car. This is called the Apparent Coxswain because, whether the driver is conscious of it or not, this car appears to other vehicles to be the leader or head of the worm. When the Apparent Coxswain changes lanes, the rest of the worm follows— not so with other, less trusted vehicles. Each car in a worm perceives the car immediately ahead of it to be the Apparent Coxswain, which leads to domino-effect lane changes. Because of this, the worm has tight integration and the ability to find a new head should something happen to the original.

When this happens the Asipetal Caterpillar morphs into the Cholinger, a worm with such a tightly integrated internal feedback system of Apparent Coxswains that it is able to transmit information from tip to tail with high fidelity. This Cholinger can slither to avoid objects in the road, twitch around slow-moving trucks, and even slip through packs of less-integrated alien worms.

There is another kind of intelligence that flows among us, between us, and through us. It is an emergent intelligence that arises from groups of individuals, even if the individuals themselves are oblivious to the particulars. We ourselves are often ignorant components of this phenomenon. Don't get me wrong, I'm not saying anyone is stupid. Except maybe my neighbor with the subwoofer. (What part of "Turn down the music, my wall is crumbling down" does he not get? Stupid jerk.) Anyway, when I say "individuals" I don't only mean people. There are millions of individual neurons bouncing around inside your brain, each one doing its own thing, but somehow, seemingly without your active participation, they have organized themselves into a lucid thought: "Let's read Biz's book." Okay, you might have had *some* input, but you get what I'm saying. They're just little neurons reacting to one another on a basic level. Individually they don't know anything, but in aggregate, they become the amazingly complex thing that is your supremely intelligent mind. How do they do that? It's both weird and cool, and it's one of the reasons I have become drawn to and immersed in the blogosphere.

Neuroscience explains how intelligence can emerge

from the chaotic free-for-all of the neurons in our heads, and Aggregate Traffic Animals lend a touch of the fantastic but no less important brand of large-scale emergent organism that the blogosphere suggests. ATAs warm us up to the idea that groups of humans can behave like neurons. Humans are only beginning to realize what other earthlings already exploit to great advantage.

Bugs and Blogs

If we could see the pheromone trail left by an ant when it finds a significant food source, we would see the biological equivalent of a blogger linking to an interesting web article. Like an ant colony, the blogosphere is a world of individuals, each doing its own thing. The pattern that emerges from this chaos is nothing short of fascinating.

Now, I'm not saying that humans and bugs are on the same intellectual plane (okay, a few people come to mind); there is obviously a big difference. But there is a key element that reduces the complexity of the human intellect to a single click.

Like tiny electric-blue insects dotting the landscape of the web, hyperlinks are the glue of our connected lives, the synapses of an intelligent web forming bridges that connect islands of knowledge to one another and create a superconsciousness, a web within the web that continues to organize itself into what we call the blogosphere through the power of feedback loops.

Ants Are Wicked Smart

I'm from Boston, but I lived in Los Angeles for about a year once. I lived on the ground floor of an apartment building. One morning I woke up and saw Bruce, my cat, staring at his food. He was transfixed. I had to find out what was so interesting about a lump of cat food left over from the night before, so I went over to check it out. Upon investigation, I discovered that the food was fuzzy, brown, and apparently alive. No, wait. It wasn't the food; it was a dense, squirming layer of ants. A thin, brown line of the tiny buggers led all the way across the apartment floor, under the back door, and out into the yard. The busy critters had discovered the cat dish and were making short work of bringing every little crumb methodically back to their colony.

Merely moving the dish to a new area didn't help. The ants would just find it again. We had to implement a new dinnertime process that involved removal and clean up as soon as Bruce was finished eating. Besides being mildly troubling, these ants were amazing. It turns out I am not alone in my fascination; there are many books on the intelligence of ant colonies. So I read up:

The intelligence of a harvester ant colony de-rives from the densely interconnected feedback between ants that encounter each other and change their behavior according to preordained rules. —Emergence

In his book, *Emergence* Steven Johnson explains how, without any individual ant knowing the big picture, a harvester colony from the Arizona desert demonstrates an aptitude for geometry. That's right folks: math. Working as one, the colony builds a cemetery at precisely the farthest point from where the ants live as well as a trash heap in such a spot that it is as far away from the colony as possible without being near the dead ants. They have solved a mathematical problem that, if I remember correctly, I got wrong on my SATs.

After an ant finds some food, it returns to the nest, dropping a chemical pheromone as it walks. When other ants detect the pheromone trail, they follow it to the food source. Then they, too, return to the nest, reinforcing the pheromone trail. Before long, there is a strong trail between the food and nest, with hundreds of ants walking back and forth.

Once the food source is gone, the ants no longer leave pheromone trails. The existing trails weaken with evaporation. As the trails weaken the ants are less likely to follow them. They begin wandering around looking for a new source of food.

Bloggers and Ants

The way the ants found the food and self-organized to bring it home is fundamental to the way bloggers behave. It's all based on the feedback loop and a few simple rules. Instead of cat food, bloggers are out foraging for online news articles or Web pages of interest. When a blogger finds something interesting, she links to it. The hyperlink here is the pheromone trail. When another blogger clicks on her link and then links to it himself, the trail is reinforced. Once there are enough links to a particular website, it shows up on the blog aggregating site Blogdex, (a site often visited by bloggers where links are ranked and measured in a variety of ways). When a link makes it to Blogdex, even more bloggers check it out and link to it. Before long, the web page is being linked to and visited by many bloggers. Then the feeding frenzy takes place. Except this time Bruce could care less.

A feeding frenzy in the blogosphere is when bloggers swarm on a particular point of interest, say, a news story. Each blogger who links to the story also adds commentary. This commentary may point out an error in the story or may contain a fact not present in the original. This collective fact-checking will often attract the attention of media giants like *The New York Times*, at which point this buzz is plucked from the blogosphere and physically distributed to millions of readers. In this way, the blogosphere demonstrates its ability to rally around a single idea, to organize itself enough to lend a unified and powerful collection of voice where there was only a dispersed few.

The blogosphere can elevate a topic enough to bring about public scrutiny and real-world change. Many voices together as one shouting YOU MUST LOOK AT THIS. This power was demonstrated in December 2002, when the blogosphere swarmed on Senate Majority Leader Trent Lott for racist comments.

> If Thurmond [who ran on a segregationist platform] had been elected president in 1948, we wouldn't have had all these problems over all these years.
> —Senator Trent Lott

The momentum that ended in Lott's resignation did not begin with the usual suspects of giant media like the *New York Times*, the *Washington Post*, or the television news networks. The controversy was instead a watershed moment for the indie subculture of blogging— filled with amateur information junkies free of the constraints of established media.

Incendiary racist comments made by Lott while attending Senator Strom Thurmond's one-hundredth birthday party on December 5, 2002, were a blip on an ABC news.com website but went unmentioned in the *Washington Post*. They were not published by the *New York Times* until five days later, after an interim period during which numerous blogs condemned the remarks, swarming on evidence of a pattern in Lott's public statements of preference toward the racist policies of the Old South.

The blog, Talking Points Memo, written by Josh Marshall, led the spontaneous campaign and refused to accept the fact that the established media were going to let this slide with the attitude that it was somehow okay because, some of our leaders go in for this kind of stuff and "It's been understood for a long time."

In the traditional big-media world, a story has a brief window of time to make an impact. If it doesn't "have legs," it doesn't get picked up. The blogosphere is different. Josh Marshall's Talking Points Memo dug up an old interview Lott had given to *Southern Partisan*, a small-circulation right-wing magazine. Other blogs, like political heavyweight Instapundit, began linking to Talking Points Memo and more evidence of Lott's hateful past until the story generated so much buzz in the blogosphere that established media picked it up. Once Paul Krugman of *The New York Times* jumped on board, this story had its legs. Trent Lott resigned as Senate majority leader later that month.

Kaycee and the Metafilter Gang

For about two years, the attractive high school, and later college, student suffering from leukemia was a very popular blogger. She was a model student, and the optimism expressed in Kaycee's online diary while she fought cancer was the stuff of legend. Kaycee's mom, Debbie, started a blog to help chronicle their lives. Last names and other information were kept private, but many people became close friends with Kaycee through e-mail, chat rooms, and even phone conversations. Her cancer was in remission, and things were looking up. That's why it was such a shock when Debbie announced that Kaycee had succumbed to the disease, more specifically, that she had died of an aneurysm. The outpouring of grief on the web was significant. Then, a lone post on the group blog Metafilter asked the unthinkable: What if this whole thing was a hoax?

Once the cat was out of the bag, a swarm intelligence set to work. The distributed investigation that these group bloggers launched was fast and brilliant. A photograph of a healthier Kaycee at high school basketball practice was available on her site. The name of the school had been edited out in a graphics program, but her shirt was clearly marked #10. When the image was opened in Photoshop, a skewed mascot was lifted and enhanced from the background. It was a lion. The bloggers tracked down the school in Kansas and dug up the basketball roster: number 10 was a girl named Julie, not Kaycee.

People began to realize that no one had ever really met Kaycee. There was no obituary to be found. A call to the local paper in the town where Kaycee supposedly lived revealed that nobody had heard of a girl dying of leukemia.

A web search for "Kaycee" yielded, among other things, a *New York Times* article about the impact of the personal computer on the social and academic lives of college students in which a girl named Kaycee Swenson was quoted. Further research with that last name turned up a family home page of one Debbie Swenson.

Kaycee's blog said that she lived in Oklahoma and moved to Kansas in 1999, and this Swenson home page had an update about moving to Kansas in 1999. Furthermore, another Metafilter user discovered that the IP address of an e-mail he had received from Kaycee before she died was from an Internet provider in Peabody, Kansas. The very place where Debbie Swenson lived.

When this and other mounting evidence was posted at Metafilter and other blogs across the web, Debbie revealed that it had all been a hoax. It turned out that Debbie does have a daughter. Her name is Kelli, and it was she and her friends who made up the imaginary Kaycee. When Debbie found out about it, she took over the masquerade and turned the fictitious Kaycee into a cancer victim, alledgedly because she wanted to tell the stories of real cancer victims she had personally known.

May 31, 2001, Thursday
METROPOLITAN DESK
Editor's Note
    An article in Circuits last Aug. 10 about the impact of the personal computer on the social and academic lives of

college students included quotations and anecdotes attributed to Kaycee Swenson, described as a prospective college freshman, on the basis of a telephone interview . . .

This month, after suspicions arose online about a separate website detailing Kaycee Swenson's fatal illness, the site's creator, Debbie Swenson, acknowledged that she had fabricated the entire tale—including Kaycee—and that she had posed as the young woman, whom she portrayed as her daughter . . .

Published: 05–31–2001, Late Edition–Final, Section A, Column 5, Page 2

Critics call blogging a form of navel gazing. Bloggers are boring and narcissistic, they say. Reading blogs is like being forced to look at your friends' scrapbooks—a bunch of meaningless, personal junk. This is often true, but these critics are missing the bigger picture. When they drive home from work, they think they're just sitting in a car. That is a sad, empty existence. Instead they could tap into the connection they are sharing with other commuters as part of a slithering, twitching aggregate traffic worm—now, that's a commute.

When people begin to realize that they have a voice on the web, that they are small but integral pieces loosely joined into intelligence greater than any one mind, then they will know that blogging is far more than navel gazing. It is the origin of what will become a whole greater than the sum of all its parts. We've seen examples of how blogs can effect real-world change, but just how exactly does this happen? What are the conditions that must come into play to launch something from the relative obscurity of a blog post to the minds of millions of people in a matter of days?

The Tipping Blog: From Idea to Epidemic

The blogosphere is a society native to the web; as such, it is subject to the phenomenon of the meme to a hyperextent. *Meme* is a word coined by author Richard Dawkins to signify a contagious idea that replicates through a society as it is propagated through person-to-person interaction. In the case of the blogosphere, however, let's call it blog-to-blog interaction.

Midnight Rider

In his book, *The Tipping Point,* Malcolm Gladwell tells the story of a spring day in Boston—April 18, 1775, to be precise—on this day, a stable boy overheard two British army officers talking to each other in low tones. Something about "Hell to pay tomorrow." The boy ran with this foreboding news to the North End home of a silversmith who listened with intent to this news. It wasn't the first time the man had heard the rumor that these soldiers were up to something.

So through the night rode Paul Revere;
And so through the night went his cry of alarm

To every Middlesex village and farm,—
A cry of defiance and not of fear,
A voice in the darkness, a knock at the door,
And a word that shall echo forevermore!
For, borne on the night-wind of the Past,
Through all our history, to the last,
In the hour of darkness and peril and need,
The people will waken and listen to hear
The hurrying hoof-beats of that steed,
And the midnight message of Paul Revere.
—Henry Wadsworth Longfellow

At 10:00 P.M. Revere mounted his horse. In two hours, he covered about thirteen miles of countryside, warning locals of the oncoming British army. He knocked on doors and shouted through windows. He was a guy on a horse, apparently with some serious news.

Then something happened. Church bells began to ring. Drums started beating. Locals began passing the information on to others. The message started spreading like wildfire. The news had traveled all the way to Worcester, forty miles west of Boston, by 5:00 A.M. the following morning. When the British began what they expected to be a surprise march toward Lexington on an unprepared countryside of clueless locals, they were met—to their astonishment—with a fierce, organized resistance.

If you went to elementary school in the United States, then you were exposed at some point to the story of Paul Revere's ride—a classic illustration of a word-of-mouth epidemic. It's easy to credit the spread of his news to the fact that it was sensational and important. However, this hypothesis does not hold up when you investigate that fateful night a little more. Why did everyone come together like that? Why wasn't Revere just "a crazy guy on a horse?" Why didn't the townspeople throw garbage at him and tell him to shut up?

> I am a wandering, bitter shade,
> Never of me was a hero made;
> Poets have never sung my praise,
> Nobody crowned my brow with bays;
> And if you ask me the fatal cause,
> I answer only, "My name was Dawes."

The poem above is a parody of Longfellow's "The Midnight Ride of Paul Revere." It was written by Helen F. Moore, and published in the *Century Magazine* in 1896. William Dawes did what Paul Revere did. He jumped on a horse and set out with the same mission, the same sensational news. Nobody remembers Dawes. In fact, the Americans were not ready for the British when they arrived in Waltham and other towns west of Boston, the area he was supposed to warn. Dawes *was* that crazy guy on a horse yelling stuff in the middle of the night. He *didn't* electrify the countryside.

One man on a horse managed to spread a message

through an entire state in a matter of hours. No e-mail. No phone. No fax. "The Tipping Point," as defined by Gladwell in his book *The Tipping Point: How Little Things Can Make a Big Difference,* is "that moment in an epidemic when a virus reaches critical mass." Gladwell also asserts that "ideas and products and messages and behaviours spread just like viruses do."

However, these things do not just mysteriously spread. They spread because of certain kinds of people, which we'll learn about in a bit. Suffice it to say, Revere was one of these types of people, Dawes was not.

Midnight Blogger

Earlier in this chapter, I compared bloggers and ants to help illustrate the power of the feedback loop in generating a feeding frenzy online and how it can give a story enough legs to effect significant social change. While feedback loops are integral to setting off a blogging frenzy, there are other elements that come into play when an idea turns into an epidemic.

In February 2002 my friend John Hiler used blogging software instead of a horse to spread his idea virus. He wrote a brilliant essay on how bloggers could game Google in such a way that they could push a particular site to the number-one result position. The concept is known as "Google bombing," and it has been used to great humorous effect against President George Bush on at least two occasions.

Google displays search results by popularity. When a particular web page has many incoming links, it has a higher PageRank on Google. When all the links to a web page contain the exact same phrase, then Google ranks that page very highly in the search results for that phrase. This is what happened to President George Bush, Jr.

Dozens of bloggers linked to a certain page with the words "Miserable Failure." This caused a Google search for "Miserable Failure" to return that page—a biography of George Bush—as the number-one result. In a world where a Google search holds as much weight as *Webster's Collegiate*, this made for a few chuckles.

My friend was the first to write extensively about this trick. At 5:00 A.M. after pulling an all-nighter, he finished his article and emailed it to a colleague for review before posting to their group blog, Corante. Then he fell asleep. John expected a few comments on his work, but he was not prepared for what happened next.

> I woke up a few hours later and hurriedly checked the server logs, anxious to see if any of my friends had linked to the article. The results stunned me: dozens of links all pointing to the article, creating a massive surge in traffic!

John woke up to a full-fledged epidemic of his own creation. His article had generated huge buzz in the blogosphere. Over the next five days more than thirty thousand people read his article; reprint rights to his piece were purchased by *Slate* (a reputable online magazine); and several other publications, including *Wired News* and the *New York Times*, picked up the story. Hundreds of thousands of people were now aware of Google bombing. Like Revere's midnight message, John's article had tipped. Why?

Anatomy of an Idea Virus

Yet another great thing about web pages is that they are very easily tracked. John turned to his web server logs to try to reconstruct the events that caused his article to become an epidemic. These were the sites that linked to him on that first day:

Number of Hits from Websites
1. 946 instapundit.blogspot.com
2. 346 www.scripting.com
3. 323 www.webmasterworld. com/forum3/2207.htm

Classic Google Bombs

Weapons of mass destruction—Internet Explorer Error look-alike page saying, "Weapons of mass destruction cannot be found."

French military victories—Google look-alike page saying, "No results found for French military victories, did you mean French military defeats?"

Miserable failure—Whitehouse.gov biography of George W. Bush

Litigious bastards—homepage of The SCO Group

Buffone—Italian prime minister Silvio Berlusconi's biography

Waffles—John Kerry's 2004 election site

4. 295 www.evhead.com

5. 175 blogdex.media.mit.edu

Sites 2 and 4 were the sites of blogging heavies Dave Winer and Evan Williams—both founders of blogging software companies with respectable amounts of daily traffic. Their early linking of the article was influential in getting it noticed in the blogosphere. But the big hits were coming in from #1 in the list, Glen Reynolds and his blog, Instapundit. In 2002, Reynolds was still a relatively young blogger compared with Winer and Williams, but he was getting enormous traffic. Reynolds was integral to this outbreak.

Gladwell explains that an idea turns into an epidemic when three types of people are involved. Glenn Reynolds, like Paul Revere, was one such person. Revere had a knack for making friends and acquaintances. As a sportsman, a card player, a theatergoer, a businessman, and a fixture at the local pub, he was the type of guy who knew a lot of people. Paul Revere was what Gladwell calls a "connector."

Connectors are *connected*. They've got lots of friends. They don't necessarily know what the hot new restaurant is, but you can bet your butt they know people who do. Once the connector finds out about the hot boîte, kiss your chance at a reservation good-bye because they'll spread that news to hundreds of friends in no time. Once it's reviewed in *Time Out*, you'll be left waiting on the sidewalk for a chance to get in with the rest of the great unwashed.

In the blogosphere, Glen Reynolds is a connector not because he knows so many people, but because so many people know him—know his blog persona, that is. Reynolds gets hundreds of thousands of visitors a day, and his blog is listed in many blogrolls. He sent 946 visitors to John's article with this quick little post:

Posted 2/27/2002 11:15:58 PM by Glenn Reynolds
I JUST RAN ACROSS this cool article on how weblogs affect Google at Ginger Stampley's site.

But the connectors have got *bupkes* without the mavens. *Maven* is a Yiddish word that means "one who accumulates knowledge." Revere was special because he was also a maven. I know what you're thinking: "I didn't know Paul Revere was Jewish. Cool, call Adam Sandler." No, Revere did not "light the menorah," but he did actively accumulate information about the British, which made him both a connector and a maven—rare in the real world but common, as it turns out, in the blogosphere. Mavens are integral to tipping because they are the ones who dig up the ideas and information.

So Reynolds got the link from this Ginger Stampley person, who is what Gladwell calls a maven, because she collects interesting links on her blog—in this case, a link to John's excellent article. Like an ant, Stampley must have been foraging online for intellectual cookie crumbs. We know she dropped blogging pheromone— the hyperlink—when she found John's article. But how had she found it? Let's dig even deeper into the foraging habits of this blogger.

> Wednesday, February 27
> Google Bombing
> This article at Corante explains how blogs have an effect out of proportion to their numbers on Google's search rankings. Personally, I think it's a Corante plot to get linked by other bloggers . . . I'm in.
> posted at 10:33 AM

John and Hylton, his blogging colleague at the time, live in New York and Boston, respectively. Ginger Stampley lives in Houston, Texas, which means she published her post at 11:33 EST—just about the same time Hylton sends out a daily e-mail to Corante subscribers. Stampley's blogroll includes Corante. So she's a regular reader and probably a subscriber of the daily e-mails— two ways she keeps track of breaking information and news. Her maven-ness is showing.

Tracing the events that lead to the diseaselike spread of John's Google-bombing article, it becomes clear that Stampley was alerted to the story either by e-mail prompt or daily surfing. She read the article and found it interesting enough to blog a link to it. Reynolds surfed over to Stampley's blog a few hours later—a happy happenstance—and also found it blogworthy. Once the link was posted to Instapundit by Reynolds, the same thing that happened during Revere's fateful ride occurred.

The news of this interesting article spread like wildfire in the blogosphere. Bloggers who regularly read Instapundit also linked to the article, reinforcing the feedback loop. Instead of church bells and drums, Blogdex—an automated pop-chart of the blogosphere—began displaying the article at the top of its list. That resulted in even more bloggers linking to it, which fanned enough flames to get the notice of the traditional media. Eventually, the story started running on news sites and even in print—on actual paper.

Just as the locals heard Revere's news and spread it to their friends and relatives, bloggers who frequent Instapundit spread the link to their regular readers. These bloggers represent the third and final type of person that Gladwell asserts is necessary in order to reach the tipping point—salesmen.

Sensational information and a popular guy on a horse successfully spreading news across the countryside is great, as far as it goes. But what about the next morning when the ragtag militia is preparing to fight a giant organized British army? Wouldn't things start to fall apart then? Wouldn't people say, "Wait a minute. Who'd we hear this from? Maybe we should go back home, get some coffee, and figure out if this is a good idea."

Peer pressure works pretty well, so there'd be a bunch of rowdy guys all psyched up for shooting some Brits with their rusty muskets. But there would also be a bunch of skeptics doubting the accuracy of the information. Someone would have to sell them on the idea: a salesman. Not the kind of salesman you picture at the car dealership, but the type of person whose character appeals to you, or has proven to you time and time again that they are worth visiting.

Readers come to trust a blogger by reading his or her posts. The ongoing nature of blogging lends context to even the shortest post: you know that this link to John's article will be good because you have learned that this blogger rarely leads you astray. In this way you are led into battle in the blogosphere. It takes a lot less selling since the worst thing that can happen is you click your browser's back button. All it takes is a gentle push from the right person and the right packaging around a link to get others infected.

Afterword

Blogging kickstarted a revolution in hyperconnectivity and communication via the web—it was the spark of life that the Internet was missing. We now know that the potential exists for everyone to have a voice, for networks to be transparent, and for a new democratic intelligence to emerge from a cacophony of individual opinions. From the blogosphere a new plane of existence has arisen—like a good version of *The Matrix*—where we are all enhanced by unlimited access to knowledge and experience and have the ability to add our own.

Computer scientists know that a bunch of cheap computers networked together are far more powerful than one expensive goliath. We've all heard the expression "many hands make light work." Zoologists have discovered that with a simple set of rules birds keep perfect formation and ants can do math. Neurologists are learning that a thought is formed in much the same way that a lively neighborhood evolves from a disparate hodgepodge of store owners, bartenders, and real estate developers. Though we have a long way to go before we fully understand how complex behavior manifests from simple units and rules, our knowledge that such emergence exists has penetrated research across wide-ranging disciplines—blogging included.

Now that we know how blogging got started and what it's all about, it's time to say good-bye. The vision Tim Berners-Lee had for the World Wide Web was that it would be readable *and* writable. Not *just* readable as the browsers of the late 1990s insisted. With the emergence of blogging the true promise of a writable web for the masses came into existence and is here to stay—but it won't be called blogging forever.

As web tools continue to become approachable, more and more individuals will use them and adapt them to their lifestyle. Bloggers will be known as the first significant portion of the world's population to flock toward this evolved version of the web and contribute to it in a way that gives back. These bloggers work the web like farmers work the land, churning it, feeding it, and harvesting the rewards it yields—and they are only at the beginning of the revolution. Blogging heralds the arrival of what Evan Williams once called "The Participatory Web." Increasingly, people are finding that their lives intersect with the web more and more. Not every person is suited to the specific activity of blogging, but as blogging becomes widespread and nearly effortless, simple, participatory web tools will get used by a huge percentage of the world.

Already, tools that are cousins to blogs, if not close family members, are filling the spaces between and around blogging. Old ideas—such as social bookmarking— whose time is now right are coming back to life. Like the abandoned desktop application John Hiler wanted to build in the early days of Xanga, social bookmarking allows people to capture, comment on, and share found items from around the web—a simple enough activity made so much more valuable when thousands of contributions are aggregated and the wisdom of a crowd emerges.

Even simpler interactions with the web such as comparison shopping and rating products by cell phone while walking through the mall make participatory web connectivity seem destined to ultimately become ubiquitous. The free flow of information *in* as well as *out* of the web together with powerful aggregation tools that leverage the power of diverse human opinion can extract a value greater than the sum of all the web's technology. Blogging has shown this to be true . . . and it's only the begining.

Resources by the Fives

5 Blogging Providers

Blogger—http://www.blogger.com

Xanga—http://www.xanga.com

Livejournal—http://www.livejournal.com

Typepad—http://www.typepad.com

20six—http://www.20six.com

5 Great Blogs

Kottke—http://www.kottke.org

BoingBoing—http://www.boingboing.net

Being Jennifer Garrett—http://www.angelfire.com/grrl/
jen_garrett

Scripting News—http://www.scripting.com

Busblog by Tony Pierce—http//www.tonypierce.com/
blog/bloggy.htm

5 Blog Pop Charts

Daypop—http://www.daypop.com
Popdex—http://www.popdex.com
Blogdex—http://www.blogdex.net
Technorati—http://www.technorati.com
Bloglines—http://www.bloglines.com/toplinks

5 Advertising Opportunities for Bloggers

AdSense—http://www.google.com/adsense
BlogAds—http://www.blogads.com
BlogSnob—http://www.blogsnob.idya.net
TextAds—http://www.textads.biz
WindowSix—http://www.windowsix.com/textads.php

5 Blog Add-ons

Side Blog—http://www.sideblog.com
News Headlines—http://www.feedrollpro.com
Blogrolling—http://www.blogrolling.com
Site Meter—http://www.sitemeter.com
Book List—http://www.allconsuming.net

Blogging Glossary

Like any revolutionary new form of communication, the blogging culture generates its fair share of jargon. Various terms mentioned throughout this book as well as a bunch of other strange or related terms have been included in this glossary for anyone hoping to blend in with the blogerati (*noun*).

Atom API

Noun. An Application Program Interface used by programmers who want to develop for blogging related services. *See also:* Atom Feed.

Atom Feed
Noun. A form of website syndication used by blogs and news aggregators to collect and display content.

Blawg
Noun. A blog primarily concerned with legal affairs; a blog written by a lawyer.

Bleg
Verb. To beg by blog usually asking information and sometimes money. One who blegs is called a "blegger" (humorous).

Blog
Noun. A personal website that provides updated headlines and news articles of other sites that are of interest to the user, also may include journal entries, commentaries, and recommendations compiled by the user; also written weblog, Web log. *Verb.* To compose and publish a blog entry.

Blog Digest
Noun. A blog that summarizes other blogs. Blog digests can be automated as in the case of kinja.com.

Blogathy
Noun. A mood characterized by a lack of interest or concern for blogging.

Blogdex

Noun. A website that serves as the pop charts of the blogosphere.

Blogerati

Noun. Intelligentsia of the blogosphere.

Blogger

1. *Noun.* A person who updates a blog. 2. *Noun.* Blogger.com, Google's blogging service.

Blogger Bash

Noun. A get-together or party arranged and attended by bloggers.

Blogging Ecosystem

Phrase. A visual or textual representation displaying the links between blogs. The system of interaction between blogs.

Bloggerel

Noun. Crudely or irregularly fashioned blog posts, especially when repeated incessantly to the point of driving away visitors.

Bloggerverse

Noun. *See* Blogosphere.

Blogistan
Noun. The sum total of political bloggers; the community of pundit blogs.

Blogiverse
Noun. See Blogosphere.

Blognoscenti
Noun. A connoisseur of blogs and blogging.

Blogorrhea
Noun. High-volume, low-quality blogging.

Blogosphere
Noun. Sum total of all blogs; the community of blogs.

Blogroll
Noun. A link-list of favorite blogs usually displayed in a blog sidebar.

Blogspot
Noun. Free blog-hosting service provided by Blogger and Google. *Also:* Blog*Spot.

Blogstipation
Noun. Writer's block for bloggers.

Blurker

Noun. A blog reader who leaves no comments and does not have a blog; a silent reader of blogs.

Bookmarklet

Noun. A link that performs an action instead of bringing up a web page. Used to help with repetitive tasks in a web browser or to save time.

Buzznet

Noun. A photo-sharing website.

Clog Blog

Noun. A blog written in Dutch.

Commenter

Noun. Someone who leaves notes in the "comment" area of a blog.

Comment Spam

Noun. Unwanted comments promoting another site.

CSS

Acronym. Stands for Cascading Style Sheets. When attached to documents, style sheets describe how the document is displayed or printed; attached to an HTML document to influence its layout when accessed via a browser.

Dead-Tree

Phrase. Newspapers, magazines, and books. Printed matter.

Edu-Blog

Noun. An education-related blog.

Ego-Surfing

Verb. Looking up one's own name in search engines to see who has linked to you and what they are saying.

Fact-Check Your Ass

Verb. To comb the Internet for clues that statements made in a blog or news article are in error.

Flame

Verb. To leave a hostile remark or blog post in an effort to start a conflict.

Flame War

Noun. The conflict that results from when a flamer flames.

Google Bomb

Verb. To intentionally use links, words, and blogs in such a way as to affect the ranking of a certain page so that it shows up prominently in Google search results for a particular search term; to game Google.

Group Blog

Noun. A blog with more than one contributor; a team blog.

Hitnosis

Noun. Unable to stop oneself from checking blog stats.

Instapundited

Transitive verb. To have your blog linked to from Instapundit.com and all the traffic that results from that action. *See also*: Slashdotted.

K-Log

Noun. A blog used for managing knowledge (usually for business).

Link Rot

Noun. When links to the intended page don't work because the documents have long since been moved or deleted.

Link Whore

Noun. A blogger who will compromise every possible principle he or she once had in order to get more bloggers to link to him/her. *Also*: link slut.

Linky Love

Noun. To link to another blogger or to link to another blogger because they have linked to you.

Meme

Noun. A contagious idea.

Meta-Blogging

Verb. To blog about blogging.

Moblog

Noun. To blog by a mobile device such as a cell phone; to blog away from the desk. Short for mobile blogging.

Movable Type

Noun. Popular blog publishing software; Movabletype.org.

Permalink

Noun. A link to an individual post in the archives of a blog that will remain intact after the post has disappeared from the blog's front page, i.e., after it has been archived.

Ping

Noun (from Packet Internet Gopher). A program that tests whether a particular network destination is online by sending a message and waiting for a response. *Verb.* To ping a site.

Propeller Head

Noun. Synonymous with computer geek. Sometimes used to describe all techies. Probably derives from science fiction fandom's tradition of propeller beanies as insignia, although nobody actually wears them. (Everyone who takes a job at Google is given a hat with a propeller on their first day.)

Progblog

Noun. A left-leaning "progressive" blog.

Pundit Blog

Noun. A blog focused mostly on news and national affairs in the media.

RSS

Noun. Stands for Really Simple Syndication, a web content syndication format.

Reciprocal Link

Noun. To link back to a blogger who has linked to your site. *See also*: Linky Love.

Referrer Logs

Noun. Statistics that show the web addresses of websites that have linked to yours. *See also*: Site Meter.

Sidebar

Noun. A column along the side of a blog usually used to publish a blogroll, a short biography, archive links, or advertising.

Sideblog

Noun. A simple, stripped-down blog included in the sidebar of a main blog and usually used to post just links with minimal commentary.

Sidebar Links

Noun. See Blogroll.

Site Meter

Noun. Sitemeter.com is a website that provides a hit-counter and statistics service; caters to bloggers.

Slashdotted

Transitive verb. To have your blog mentioned and linked to or from Slashdot.org. *See also:* Instapundited.

Tech Blog

Noun. A blog focused on a technical subject.

Trackback

Noun. Provides a method of notification between websites to bring related posts together on a page; a passive commenting system.

Troll

Verb. To publish provocative comments or posts in an effort to provoke an angry response; to goad. *Noun.* A person who trolls.

Warblog

Noun. A blog that sprung up after September 11, 2001, to cover reaction and related events such as terrorism, military operations, and Middle East conflicts; a subset of pundit blogs; a political blog.

WaSP

Acronym. Stands for "The Web Standards Project," a grassroots coalition fighting for standards that ensure simple, affordable access to web technologies for all.

Weblog

Noun. See Blog.

WYSIWYG

Acronym. Stands for "What You See Is What You Get." Pronounced *wiz-ee-wig.* Blogging providers such as Blogger provide the option of using a built-in WYSIWYG HTML editor for composing and styling blog posts. Knowledge of HTML is not necessary.

XML

Stands for Extensible Markup Language; a flexible way to create standard information formats and share both the format and the data on the web.

Acknowledgments

I've heard that some writers take time off from work to write a book. That must be nice. This book was written during the nights and weekends of my first few months at Google directly following a cross-country drive. I'd like to thank my coworkers for putting up with all my whining during that time. Jennifer Garrett—fellow blogger, friend, and coconspirator—helped me during the primordial phase of this book before I headed out West. Thanks for talking about ants with me during lunch, Jen.

Special acknowledgment must go to Steve Snider for putting me in touch with the coolest editor ever, Elizabeth Beier—who somehow managed to keep me focused with the strategic implementation of e-mail and FedEx. Thanks, Elizabeth, and thanks to friends and family who had to put up with me while I wrote this book, *cough* Livy. A full allotment of e-props to Wil Wheaton for contributing a great foreword, and of course: word to my cat, Bruce.

ACKNOWLEDGMENTS

Index